AF428433

THE SECRET LANGUAGE OF P.A.W.S.

Decoding Your Cat's Personality and Discovering What It Reveals About You

J.W. KINCAID

Ben G. Publishing
Richmond, Virginia

Edited by Colette Chalier

Cover design: 99 Designs

Interior design: Publishing Services

Photos: ChatGPT or as attributed

Library of Congress Cataloging-in-Publication Data

Kincaid, J.W.

The Secret language of PAWS: decoding your cat's personality and discovering what it reveals about you / J.W. Kincaid.

p. cm.

Includes bibliographical references and index.

Paperback 979-8-9945221-4-1

Hardcover 979-8-9945221-5-8

Ebook 979-8-9945221-3-4

1. Cats—Behavior. 2. Cats. 3. Animal—Behavior. I. Title.

636.8—dc22

Summary: *The Secret Language of PAWS* presents a practical framework for understanding cat personality types and the emotional meanings behind common feline behaviors. Blending behavioral insight with reflective storytelling, the book explores the human–cat bond and how cats often mirror their owners' emotional states.

Legal Notice

Disclaimer Notice

ACKNOWLEDGEMENT

This book is dedicated to Rhu (aka Rhubie), my wife's beloved Adventurer cat and companion through so many chapters of life. Rhu was born deaf, she was pure white, with one blue eye and one green eye.

Thank you Rhu, for the comfort you gave so freely and the fun you brought into our home. You traveled the world with us, adapting with curiosity, reminding us that presence

Rhu, 2021

matters more than place. In moments of stress and uncertainty (ie, Zambia), you offered steady companionship, warmth, and a constant presence. You lived with us for many years, did your job simply by being you, and when it was time, you left this world leaving a huge hole in our hearts. This work carries your spirit of loyalty, adventure, and sneaky antics, and we are forever grateful for the love you gave.

🖤

APPENDICES – SCAN QR CODE TO DOWNLOAD

Appendix 1: Worksheets

Appendix 2: Dictionary of Feline Language

Appendix 3: 7-Day plan to understand your cat's personality profile

Appendix 4: How to use the PAWS framework to discover your cat's personality style

Appendix 5: 30-Day companion journal: Learning the language of PAWS

Appendix 6: 30-Day plan to understand your cat's language

Appendix 7: Quick reference: Blended PAWS personalities

Appendix 8: Home design quick guide: Creating harmony for every PAWS type

CONTENTS

INTRODUCTION

LISTENING TO THE LANGUAGE
OF WHISKERS AND HEARTBEATS

If you've ever lived with a cat, you already know that they have their own quiet way of running the world. They don't bark for attention or wag their tails for constant approval. They are present, observing, judging, choosing their moments. One glance, one blink, one slow stretch across the couch (or across your face) can communicate more than a thousand words ever could.

And yet, for all our fascination, cats remain wrapped in mystery. They've been called aloof, unpredictable, and even untrainable. Some people assume cats don't feel as deeply as dogs, that their affection is conditional, and that their loyalty is fleeting. But those of us who share our lives with cats know otherwise. We've seen their emotional intelligence in the way they comfort us during hard days, the way they watch over us from the windowsill, or how they greet us at the door with a meow that sounds suspiciously like "welcome back."

The truth is simple and profound: cats love differently, not less.

This book was born out of years of observing, researching, and simply living with cats, not just through behavior charts and veterinary notes, but through everyday life. Both my wife and I grew up in homes with beloved cats. I began to see patterns in how different cats expressed their affection, curiosity, and calm. Some guarded their homes like quiet sentinels; others turned every box, curtain, and shadow into an adventure. Some radiated peace like furry philosophers, while others seemed to feel everything: your mood, your energy, your silence, as if it were their own. As I'm trained in DISC personality assessment, I wanted to apply the principles of personality assessment to cats. This is my own assessment system and I named it, appropriately, P.A.W.S.

Cats show clear patterns in how they act and how they connect with you, and my P.A.W.S. framework gives you a simple way to see these patterns. P.A.W.S. represents four types of cats, each with its own style of emotion and behavior.

The four types of P.A.W.S.:

- The Protector
- The Adventurer
- The Wise One
- The Sensitive Soul

Each type is beautiful in its own way, and none is better than the others. Together, they paint a portrait of the feline spirit that is complex, emotional, and endlessly fascinating. The more I thought about and studied these personalities, the more I saw something even more remarkable: they reflect us.

Our cats often mirror our emotional states. The anxious person might find comfort in a calm, Wise cat. The restless spirit might attract an Adventurer. The tender-hearted may bond with a Sensitive Soul.

In a quiet, almost mystical exchange, cats teach us the lessons we most need: patience, curiosity, resilience, and most importantly - unconditional presence.

What Cats Teach Us About Ourselves

We often think of ourselves as our pets' caretakers. We feed them, groom them, and protect them from harm. But look closely, and you'll see that they take care of us too, not with words or rules, but with energy.

They remind us to pause, to listen, and to live in the moment. They teach us that gentleness can be strength and that silence can be communication. They model boundaries without apology and affection without neediness. Ok, sometimes neediness.

When you begin to see your cat through the P.A.W.S. lens, you'll notice how their personality influences yours, how their steadiness soothes you, their curiosity awakens you, their serenity calms you, and their sensitivity humbles you.

This book is about that exchange: the subtle, powerful relationship between human and feline souls.

Why I Wrote This Book: A Journey from Mystery to Meaning

My earliest memory of cats in the home goes back to when I was three years old. Some were adopted on purpose, others showed up as strays, and every one of them became part of our family. I watched them give birth, raise their kittens, claim their spots in the house, and at times I even witnessed their deaths.

Over the years, dozens of cats came and went, each with a distinct personality. Dozens may seem like a lot, but growing up on a small Caribbean island, our yard was an open space for cats to come and go. Some stayed for years and became a part of the family. Some, like Maribeth, were affectionate and cuddly. Others, like Molly, were silent observers. Jacko hissed at strangers, while Sambo fiercely guarded his territory. Marco Polo, one of my in-laws' cats, was even named for his adventurous ways! These behaviors were visible, but they only scratched the surface.

Despite living with cats for over 40 years, I never truly understood them. They remained a mystery: complex, layered, and often misunderstood, especially when compared to the emotional transparency of our dogs.

I didn't set out to write a book about cats.

I set out to understand them because of the huge space they occupy in our hearts. I also wrote it for my future grandchildren, as a way to connect and document the creatures that have impacted my life and my family's life so profoundly. I created the P.A.W.S. framework to connect scholarly research to every day life. This book can be as insightful, serious, or lighthearted as you make it. I wrote it for cat lovers everywhere who cherish their companions as much as my family and I do.

Each cat I have lived with revealed unique emotional traits, such as loyalty, boldness, calmness, and empathy. They expressed themselves not with words, but with quiet glances, gentle or not so gentle paw-taps, slow blinks, and sudden sprints. I began to see their individuality as a mix of instinct and temperament: distinct, consistent, and rich with small details.

From this realization, the **P.A.W.S. Framework** was born:

- **Protector:** Loyal guardians of home and heart
- **Adventurer:** Bold explorers who chase joy
- **Wise One:** Calming presences rooted in stillness
- **Sensitive Soul:** Empaths in fur, tuned to our emotions

These four archetypes offer a language for decoding feline behavior and, perhaps, a unique new way to understand your own.

This book blends personality insight with real-life stories to help you recognize who your cat truly is beneath the surface. It's not just a guide to feline behavior; it's a mirror into connection, presence, and trust.

It's love, made visible.

MEET THE CATS BEHIND P.A.W.S.

Before we move forward into tools, observations, and application, it's important to pause and meet some of the cats who shaped this framework in the first place. P.A.W.S. did not emerge from theory alone, but from years of living alongside four very different types of cats whose personalities were as distinct and consistent as any I've seen in people. They weren't case studies or concepts; they were my companions (shared with my siblings!). Through their behaviors, boundaries, fears, and forms of affection, they quietly revealed patterns that would later become the foundation of this work. What follows is not an introduction to archetypes, but an introduction to the cats themselves, whose lives and lessons gave P.A.W.S. its heart. Regrettably I don't have any actual pictures from my childhood – of myself or my cats --as my family didn't have a camera. Therefore, the pictures in this book from open source internet or AI generation (attributed as labeled) are the closest I could find to my memory.

🐾 Sambo - The Protector

Sambo's likeness

Sambo was named by my brother Colin. He was all grey and had a solid, muscular build with a dense black coat, piercing golden eyes, and a strong, controlled tail that signaled quiet authority. Calm and steady, Sambo felt responsible for maintaining safety and order, stepping forward when protection was needed and staying close when reassurance mattered. He taught me that strength was often silent and that leadership was rooted in presence and reliability.

🐾 Maribeth - The Adventurer

Maribeth's likeness

Maribeth came into our lives roughly when I was 10 years old. She had a sleek, short-haired coat in warm orange tabby tones, with bold stripes, bright amber eyes, and a long, expressive tail that often stood tall. She moved through the world with curiosity and confidence. Exploration energized her, and she seemed to learn by doing - leaping first and adapting quickly. Maribeth reminded me that growth came from curiosity, courage, and the willingness to step into the unknown.

🐾 Jacko - The Wise One

Jacko stands out clearly in my memory as he was one of my companions through high school. He had a medium-length tabby coat in muted brown and gray tones, thoughtful amber eyes, and a gently curved tail that rarely flicked in haste. He moved slowly and deliberately, observing before responding and choosing stillness when others rushed. Jacko reminded me that wisdom grew through reflection,

Jacko's likeness

balance, and the courage to pause before we moved.

🐾 Molly - The Sensitive Soul

Molly lived a long and happy life with our family. She had a soft gray-and-white, medium-to-long plush coat with subtly blended tones, large expressive green eyes, and a full, fluffy tail she often wrapped close when resting. Deeply attuned to moods and subtle shifts, she restored herself in quiet, familiar spaces and

Molly's likeness

offered comfort through calm presence rather than noise or demand. Molly reminded me that sensitivity was not fragility, but awareness, empathy, and emotional depth.

How to Use This Book

This book was designed to meet you wherever you are in your relationship with your cat. You may choose to read it straight through from beginning to end, allowing the ideas to build naturally from one chapter to the next. You may also prefer to jump ahead to the chapters that immediately catch your interest - perhaps a personality type that already feels familiar.

That said, the most rewarding approach is to begin by understanding the **P.A.W.S. Framework** as a whole. Before focusing on individual traits or behaviors, take time to identify your cat's primary personality style or combination of styles. This foundation will help everything else in the book make sense and prevent common misunderstandings about why your cat behaves the way they do.

To support this process, the worksheets in Appendix 1 are an essential part of the book, not an optional extra. They will guide you in observing patterns, interpreting behaviors, and identifying your cat's unique P.A.W.S. profile. Use them slowly and thoughtfully, returning to them as your understanding deepens.

You'll also find a dictionary of feline language in Appendix 2 designed to help you translate common behaviors, signals, and responses. This reference can be revisited often, especially when something feels confusing or unexpected.

If you are a quick reader, consider slowing down. This is not a book meant to be skimmed for tips or tricks. Its purpose is not simply to give you more information about your cat, but to help you learn how to communicate, interpret, and respond in ways that strengthen trust over time.

Ultimately, this book is about strengthening a relationship with a lifelong companion, one rooted in understanding, respect, and emotional awareness. The more intentionally you move through these pages, the more meaningful that connection can become.

A FINAL WORD
BEFORE WE BEGIN

There's a saying that "dogs come when called; cats take a message and get back to you."

That might be true, but what a message it is.

Cats remind us that connection doesn't have to be loud or obvious to be real. Love can be quiet. Loyalty can look like stillness and joy can live in a single purr.

So, as you read this book, I invite you to slow down. Observe your cat not as a pet, but as a companion spirit with lessons to share. Listen to the soft rhythm of their paws against the floor, the hum of their breath, and the steady pulse of contentment in their chest.

Because within every cat lies a story, not just who they are, but about who we can become when we finally learn to listen.

CHAPTER 1

THE LANGUAGE OF PAWS

WHY CATS ARE MORE COMPLEX THAN WE THINK

If you think your cat is just "being a cat," think again. Behind those quiet stares, twitching tails, and deliberate silences is a rich emotional life most people miss entirely. Cats aren't necessarily mysterious. We just haven't been paying close enough attention. This chapter explains why everything you thought you knew about cat behavior is probably wrong and shows you how to finally start understanding your cat for who they really are.

Rethinking the "Cold Cat" Stereotype

Cats have long been described as aloof, uncaring, or indifferent. That reputation isn't based on truth, but on misunderstandings. They didn't evolve to obey or please. They evolved to observe, adapt, and respond quietly. That doesn't mean they don't feel; it means they think in a way most people fail to recognize.

What looks like detachment is often just emotional restraint, and what seems like disinterest is caution, sensitivity, or even love shown on their terms. Cats watch everything, remember routines, and respond to your moods. They know when something is off, and they often come closer when it is, not with fanfare, but with presence.

A cat that follows you silently from room to room is saying more than it seems. The one who sits nearby but doesn't engage is giving you space while offering connection, and their way of bonding may be subtle, but it's deliberate and deeply personal.

New research backs this up. Studies in feline cognition show that cats form secure emotional attachments with their humans, similar to the bonds formed by dogs or even young children. They just show it differently.

Emotion in Motion: How Cats Communicate Without Words

Every move your cat makes is a message. Their entire body is a communication tool. For instance, a tail that twitches fast can signal overstimulation, while a slow, sweeping motion may show interest. Straight up often means 'confidence' or 'greeting'. Also, flattened ears suggest discomfort, while half-closed eyes or slow blinks indicate trust and calm.

When they are still, which seems to be "doing nothing," it often means they are processing. Stillness is rarely neutral; it is observation, maybe tension, comfort, or anticipation. And when a cat touches you, like gently (or not gently) placing a paw on your arm, that is intentional. Cats use touch selectively, and when they initiate it, it usually means something.

Sound plays a role, too. Purring doesn't always mean happiness. It can also be self-soothing or even a request for reassurance. Chirps, trills, and subtle vocalizations are part of a social language cats use with those they trust.

Learning to "speak cat" means slowing down, noticing small shifts, and giving each signal its due weight.

Personality Isn't Just a Human Thing

Cats aren't one-size-fits-all. Each one has a personality that shapes how they interact with the world. For too long, animal personality has been dismissed as people projecting human traits onto animals. That view is outdated.

We now know that animals, including cats, have distinct traits. These affect their comfort zones, attachment styles, and emotional range.

Some cats are bold and curious. Others prefer consistency and quiet. Others hiss then run and hide. Some crave interaction, while others bond best through shared space. Recognizing these traits means that you are meeting your cat where they are, rather than putting them in some specific box or category.

When you understand your cat's emotional wiring, you stop expecting them to behave like dogs or like past cats you've known, and you begin to read them clearly, on their own terms.

Observation Is Connection

If you want a stronger relationship with your cat, start by paying attention. Not casually, but intentionally. Observation is how cats understand the world, including you, and it should be how you understand them, too.

Cats don't over-communicate. They don't explain themselves through constant gestures or noise. Instead, they signal in consistent and repeatable behavioral patterns that tell you exactly how they feel, if you're paying close enough attention.

What may seem minor or random is often a clear emotional signal:

- Where they sit is less about comfort and more about security, attachment, and territory.
- When they approach, they can show curiosity, openness, or a bid for interaction.
- When they withdraw, it might be a sign of overstimulation, uncertainty, or a request for space.
- How they react to your voice or energy shows how closely they monitor your emotional state and how much it matters to them.

These behavioral patterns are not quirks but habits built from observation and memory. Your cat is constantly reading the environment, including you. They remember tone, patterns, even how you respond to their cues, and that's how trust is built, not through control, but through mutual awareness.

When you notice your cat's habits and adjust your own behavior in response, you're showing respect. You're saying, *I see you.* Cats notice that. Over time, your cat learns that you're someone who listens, not just with words, but with attention.

Observation doesn't mean watching from a distance. It means tracking patterns, context, and consistency. It means noticing when something is slightly different, like posture, placement, or pacing, and understanding it's a message.

It's how you learn what your cat needs to feel safe, and how you earn their trust without forcing it. In this way, observation becomes emotional fluency and shared language. In a relationship with a cat, observation isn't passive but the most active form of love they recognize.

Why You Need a Framework

Feline behavior is often subtle and highly individual, which makes it easy to misread. Without a structure for understanding what you're seeing, small signals can be missed or misinterpreted. That's where a framework becomes useful.

After years of closely observing cats across different environments, one consistent pattern emerged: cats tend to fall into distinct emotional styles. These weren't rigid categories or personality "types" in the way people often use them. Instead, they are consistent behavioral profiles shaped by how each cat processes emotion, perceives safety, and connects with others.

Some cats lead with boldness and curiosity. Others rely on quiet observation. Some guard their space and routines fiercely, while others show deep sensitivity to shifts in energy or tone. These responses were not random but reflected deeper emotional patterns that shaped the cat's engagement with the world.

To make sense of these patterns and help people respond with more clarity and empathy, I developed the **P.A.W.S. Framework,** a practical system for identifying your cat's emotional orientation and understanding how to support them more effectively.

Each letter in P.A.W.S. represents a different emotional style:

- **Protector**: defensive, loyal, and deeply attuned to territory and routine
- **Adventurer**: bold, curious, often energetic, and socially outgoing
- **Wise One**: observant, cautious, comfortable with distance and independence

- **Sensitive Soul**: emotionally reactive, intuitive, easily overwhelmed by change

This system is not meant to put your cat in a box. It's about meeting them where they are, recognizing how they communicate their emotional needs, and building a relationship based on insight rather than assumption.

In the chapters ahead, you'll learn how to identify your cat's emotional orientation and how to interact with them in a way that builds trust, reduces stress, and strengthens your connection.

The first step is awareness. The next step is understanding what those subtle behaviors are really telling you. The **P.A.W.S. Framework** is your guide for doing both.

As we begin to see cats not as unpredictable enigmas but as emotionally expressive individuals, a question naturally arises: if every cat communicates so uniquely, how can we better understand them?

That question led to the creation of the **P.A.W.S. Framework**, a way to map the core personality patterns that shape how each cat perceives, feels, and interacts with the world. In the next chapter, we'll explore how these four distinct styles emerged from years of observation and research, and how recognizing your cat's style can transform the way you connect, train, and live together.

CHAPTER 2

THE FOUR PERSONALITY STYLES FRAMEWORK OF FELINE BEHAVIOR

Four fundamental feline personality types or temperaments can help us better understand how a cat interacts with the world. To visualize these styles, imagine a circle divided into four equal parts, like slices of a pie. Each piece represents a distinct personality type, and together, they form an interconnected system. No  type exists in isolation; they relate, contrast, and complement one another.

To grasp the heart of this P.A.W.S. Framework, let's begin by dividing our circle horizontally into two halves. This first division represents one of the most essential distinctions in feline personality: **energy expression**.

- The **top half** of the circle represents **expressive** cats - those who are actively engaged with their environment. These cats tend to be outward-facing, high-energy, and quick to interact.

- The **bottom half** represents more **reserved** cats. These felines are quieter, more inward-focused, and tend to control their space through observation and consistency rather than outward activity.

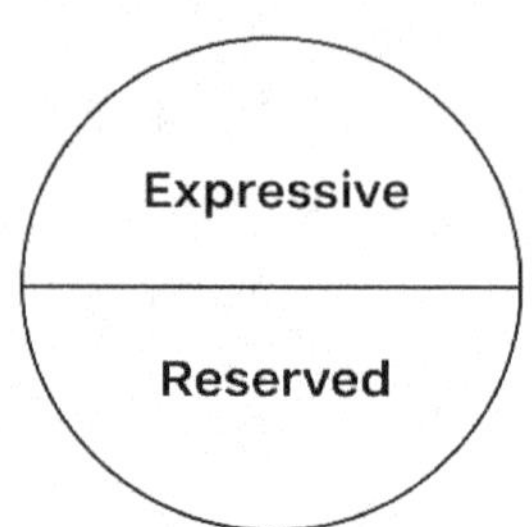

Now, imagine cutting the pie **vertically**, creating a second axis. This split gives us another important distinction: **focus of engagement**.

- On the **left side** are cats that are more **environment-oriented**. These cats are primarily driven by territory, safety, structure, and their relationship to space.
- On the **right side** are cats who are more **people-oriented**. These cats thrive on connection, bonding, emotional attunement, and relationships.

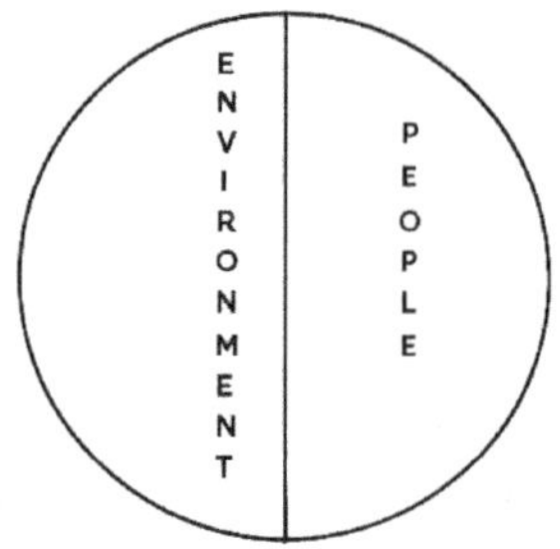

By combining these two axes: **Expressive vs. Reserved** and **Environment-Oriented vs. People-Oriented,** we arrive at four unique yet related feline personality types. Each one occupies its own quadrant of the circle, offering a clearer, more compassionate understanding of how cats behave, bond, and express themselves.

Explaining the P.A.W.S. Personality Framework in Depth

Cats express personality in subtle, complex, and often misunderstood ways. Unlike humans or even dogs, their social and emotional cues are usually quiet, delivered through posture, space, gaze, and energy rather than overt gestures. The **P.A.W.S. Personality Framework** is designed to help decode this quiet language by mapping feline behavior across two foundational dimensions:

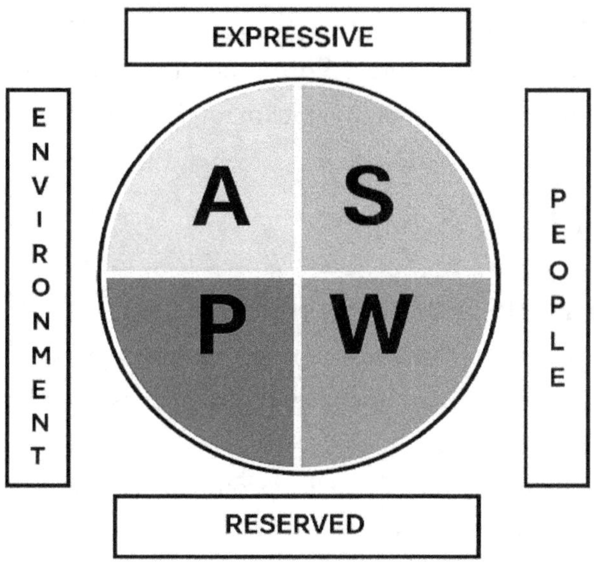

1. **Energy Expression:** Whether a cat tends to be more **expressive** (outgoing, reactive, emotionally visible) or **reserved** (calm, observant, internally regulated).
2. **Engagement Focus:** Whether a cat is more **environment-oriented** (focused on territory, space, objects, and

movement) or **people-oriented** (tuned into human presence, emotions, and social bonding).

These two axes intersect to form four distinct feline personality styles, each with its own core drive, behavioral language, and emotional blueprint.

Cats express personality in different ways, and the P.A.W.S. model helps us make sense of them by organizing feline behavior across two core traits: how expressive or reserved they are, and whether they're more focused on their environment or the people around them. These dimensions combine to form four distinct personality styles: Protector, Adventurer, Wise One, and Sensitive Soul, each revealing a unique way cats love, learn, and relate.

The Four P.A.W.S. Styles

- **Protector** (Reserved + Environment-Oriented):
  - Quiet, watchful, and deeply loyal. These cats thrive in structured environments and often act as the silent guardians of the home.
- **Adventurer** (Expressive + Environment-Oriented):
  - Curious, energetic, and playful. Adventurers crave novelty, enjoy challenges, and bring vibrant life to their surroundings.
- **Wise One** (Reserved + People-Oriented):
  - Calm, grounding, and emotionally stabilizing. Wise Ones build trust slowly but offer deep companionship through stillness and presence.

- **Sensitive Soul** (Expressive + People-Oriented):
    - Affectionate, intuitive, and empathetic. These cats are emotionally open and deeply responsive to the feelings of the humans around them.

Note: *For visual clarity, styles P.A.W.S. are arranged by temperament flow, not acronym order.*

Each style reflects a different way cats love, learn, protect, and play. Some are energized by exploration, others by closeness. Some create harmony through silence, while others express joy with vocal trills or confident leaps. These four categories may seem generalized, but as you read you'll see where your own cat fits in.

What makes this framework powerful is its ability to see beyond behavior and recognize personality. It moves us from reacting to what a cat does to understanding why they do it.

And once we understand, we can connect more deeply, better support their needs, and build a more compassionate bond with the animals we share our lives with. Cats are not just pets but individuals with emotional worlds as vivid and varied as our own.

CHAPTER 3

THE "P" TYPE PERSONALITY - THE PROTECTOR

Style: The Protector (Reserved + Environment-Oriented)

The letter **"P"** stands for **Protective, Patient, Perceptive, Private, and Persistent** in these cats. Protector cats are quiet but influential figures in the home. They rely on stability, routine, and a strong sense of space. They don't seek constant affection or attention. Instead, they offer a calm, grounding presence that helps regulate the environment and those within it.

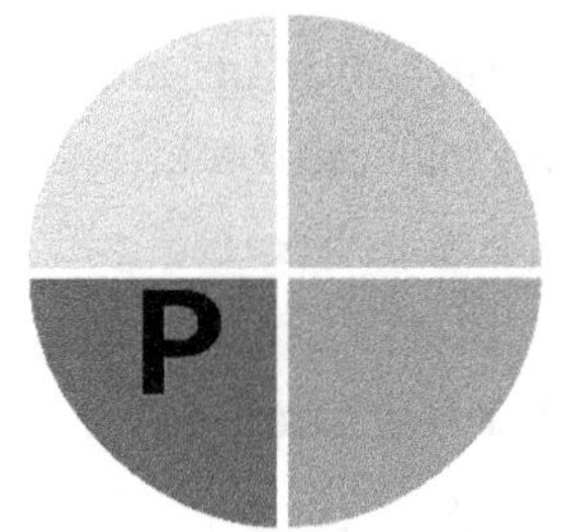

These cats typically form strong bonds with a select few and show affection through closeness without crowding. You'll find them positioned just near enough to keep an eye on you, often choosing resting spots like doorways, corners, or high perches. From there, they observe and assess. Every movement is deliberate. Their loyalty is steady, not showy.

When tension arises, whether from visitors, loud noise, or other animals, they don't panic. They respond with quiet authority: a sharp stare, a low sound, or a shift in body language. They protect not just their home, but their relationships. Their emotional presence is subtle but powerful.

Primary Motive

They move through life with a steady instinct to create safety, maintain stability, and guard what matters to them. They shape their space with calm assurance, constant presence, and quiet devotion.

Instinct in Action: How the Protector Keeps Watch

Protector cats express their instinct for safety through positioning, pattern, and presence rather than noise or confrontation. Their behaviors are deliberate and often misunderstood because they are subtle rather than dramatic.

One of the clearest signs of a Protector is their tendency to place themselves in pathways, lying in

Molly's likeness

doorways, sitting at the top of stairs, or positioning their body between you and an entry point. This is not obstruction or possessiveness. It is perimeter control: monitoring movement, sound, and energy before it reaches those they are bonded to.

Many Protectors circle their resting spot before settling and may delay eating until the household is calm. These behaviors reflect vigilance, not anxiety; for them, rest comes only after safety is confirmed.

At night, Protectors often patrol familiar routes or move objects to specific locations, performing quiet checks that ensure the environment remains secure and unchanged.

Because these behaviors are not overtly affectionate, Protectors are sometimes misread as controlling or distant. In truth, they are communicating something simple:

I am responsible for safety.

Their instinct is not to be noticed, but to create quiet stability so others can rest.

Protector's Motto: *"I keep watch so that you can rest."*

This is the cat that positions itself near the door when you're away, curls up beside your bed when you're ill, and silently appears when something feels off. Their presence is less about possession and more about protecting you, the home, and the emotional energy in their environment.

Traits of a Protector-Type Cat

Protector-type cats are defined by the following qualities, each contributing to their role as the quiet guardians of the household:

- *Steady routines:* Protector cats thrive when life follows a predictable rhythm. Regular feeding times, consistent sleeping spots, and familiar household patterns help them feel grounded and secure. Sudden changes, such as new furniture, unexpected visitors, and schedule disruptions, can unsettle them because routine is their emotional anchor. Stability allows them to relax, observe, and focus on keeping their environment safe.

- *Vigilant awareness:* These cats are always on the lookout. Their senses are dialed up, not in a nervous way, but in a deeply attuned way. They'll notice the shift in your tone before you finish a sentence, the sound of footsteps outside before you hear the knock, or an object out of place when they enter the room. Nothing escapes the Protector's quiet surveillance.

- *Subtle affection*: Affection from a Protector is gentle, understated, and rooted in presence rather than performance. They may sit near you instead of on you, rest at the foot of the bed instead of in your arms, or give a soft head bump before returning to their lookout position. To them, closeness is love. Their affection is quality over quantity in the form of quiet touches, soft purring, and the simple act of choosing to be near you.

- *Territorial loyalty*: Protectors form strong bonds with people and with places. Their home and the people within it are their territory. They will stand guard over doorways, sleep facing entry points, or insert themselves between you and a stranger without hesitation. When someone enters the space, they assess whether this person belongs. Their loyalty isn't possessive but protective.

- *Calm presence:* Their greatest gift is their ability to bring peace simply by being there. When emotions like stress, sadness, or tension rise, the Protector stays grounded. They may sit near you when you're overwhelmed or quietly appear during challenging moments.

Have You Ever Noticed This Behavior?

Have you ever noticed…

…how some cats choose to sit between you and the door, even when no one is there? They aren't in the way. They're positioning themselves where they can see first, hear first, and respond first.

Have you ever noticed…

…a cat who waits until the house is quiet before fully settling down? While others sleep, they remain alert just a little longer, only relaxing once everyone feels safe and accounted for.

Have you ever noticed…

…how certain cats walk the same path through the house each evening, night after night? Not from restlessness, but from routine patrol, checking familiar spaces, listening for changes, and making sure everything is as it should be.

How They Bond: Love Rooted in Loyalty

For the Protector, bonding is not something rushed or freely given. It is a sacred, intentional process built quietly, layer by layer, over time. A need for constant closeness does not drive these cats; instead, a deep-rooted sense of loyalty and emotional responsibility does. For them, trust is earned, not assumed. And once it is given, it runs deep and unwavering.

Their love is not flashy or loud but felt in their presence. In their world, affection is measured not by how close they are physically, but by how present they are emotionally. Once bonded, a Protector will often choose one or two humans as their "inner circle," quietly devoting themselves to those individuals with steadfast consistency.

Their bond is not built through dramatic displays of affection, but through subtle, meaningful actions that communicate, *"I am here. I see you. I've got you."*

What Protector Bonding Looks Like

- *They follow you from room to room, silently:* They don't meow or demand attention. They don't need to be held or touched. They stay close, not to be seen, but to see you. Their silent trailing is not curiosity but loyalty in motion.
- *They sit beside you, facing outward:* This is one of the Protector's most signature behaviors. While other cats might curl up in your lap, the Protector prefers to sit nearby, often with their back to you or angled outward, watching the room. In their minds, your safety is their priority, and their affection manifests as guarding the perimeter.
- *They position themselves between you and perceived threats:* whether it's the front door, a new guest, or a loud sound, Protectors will often instinctively move to place their bodies between you and the source. They are not aggressive but are calculated shields, acting as silent sentinels in times of uncertainty.
- *They check in during moments of distress:* When you're upset, overwhelmed, or ill, you may notice them appear and sit quietly nearby, sometimes just watching, other times brushing gently against you. They don't impose comfort; instead, they offer it calmly and respectfully.

This type of bonding may go unnoticed by those who expect cats to be cuddly, vocal, or physically clingy. But for the Protector, bonding is built on trust, not touch. Their loyalty is shown through consistency, presence, and an unspoken promise: "I'm here when you need me, even if you don't say a word."

They become your quiet guardian, choosing their favorite spots not for comfort, but for proximity and protection. And in time, you may find that their silent companionship speaks louder than a thousand meows.

Strengths of the Protector: Anchors in a Shifting World

Protector-type cats may not seek the spotlight, but their presence is felt in powerful and consistent ways. Their strength lies not in what they do loudly, but in how they anchor a home's emotional tone through subtle yet impactful behaviors.

The Protector shows their value through three core strengths that shape the emotional climate of the home and influence how everyone else feels and behaves around them.

Grounding Energy

Protector cats radiate a calming presence that brings emotional balance to their environment. Their energy is steady and unshakable, and just being near them can make a space feel safer and more centered. When the household is chaotic, their calm presence acts as a silent reminder to slow down and breathe. Whether they're curled in a nearby corner or simply sitting in a doorway, they exude a kind of quiet authority that naturally reduces stress in those around them. They are, quite literally, the emotional ground wire of the home.

Alert Protectiveness

One of the Protector's most notable strengths is their unmatched awareness. These cats are highly attuned to the tiniest changes in their surroundings, be it a shift in routine, a new visitor, a strange noise, or even a subtle change in your mood. Their alert protectiveness isn't born out of fear, but rooted in loyalty and a desire to maintain harmony and safety in their environment.

Empathetic Attunement

Protector cats often possess an uncanny ability to tune in to the emotional states of those around them. They seem to know when something isn't right. Whether you're anxious, grieving, or simply tired, they'll quietly appear beside you, not to fix, but to witness. This is the beauty of their empathy: it is gentle, noninvasive, and always respectful of your space.

They won't demand to be petted or jump into your lap unless you invite them. But they will sit close enough so that you feel their presence like a heartbeat beside your own, offering unspoken reassurance. Their emotional intelligence is subtle but profound.

Area for Growth: When Loyalty Turns to Over-Vigilance

Because a need for control and security drives Protectors, they can:

- Become hyper-alert or anxious in unstable environments.
- Overreact to visitors or changes in routine.
- Withdraw or isolate when overwhelmed or when their environment becomes chaotic.

They may also become territorial or even passive-aggressive if they feel their space is being invaded, particularly by other animals or new household dynamics.

Don't Correct This - Support It This Way

Instinct: Guard space, people, and territory

Don't correct this…

- Sleeping in doorways or hallways
- Sitting upright instead of curling up
- Positioning themselves between you and visitors
- Monitoring rooms rather than settling in one spot

Support it this way:

- Place a cat bed or mat near entry points so they can rest while remaining alert
- Allow clear sightlines instead of forcing cozy hiding spots
- Acknowledge their presence calmly when guests arrive— don't push them aside
- Keep household routines predictable; stability reinforces their sense of control

Why it works:

You're honoring their role as sentinel instead of removing it.

Play Style

A Protector's play style is focused and intentional rather than spontaneous, driven by a desire to maintain control, follow routine, and defend their territory through purposeful, measured interactions.

Preferred Toys & Games:

- Hunting-style wand toys (especially prey-like: mice, feathers, birds)
    - ○ → Helps them simulate protective instincts
- Tunnel toys or "guard stations"
    - ○ → Allow them to observe and "patrol" while still engaging
- Food puzzles with guarding potential
    - ○ → Triggers territorial satisfaction
- Window perches with bird feeders outside
    - ○ → Lets them "watch over" the outside world in calm focus

Keep their toys in specific locations to support their need for routine. Surprise or chaotic play can cause stress.

Creating Stability for the Protector

To support a Protector's emotional and behavioral health:

- Keep a consistent routine – feeding times, cleaning, play—consistency is key.
- Create safe zones – high perches, quiet rooms, or cozy hideaways where they can retreat.

- Introduce change slowly – whether it's new people, pets, or furniture, give them time to adjust.
- Respect their boundaries – physical affection should be on their terms.
- Offer quiet bonding rituals – brushing, slow blinking, or sitting together in silence.

Protector Love Language

Protector cats express love through quiet consistency. They don't express affection with flashy gestures; they show it by being there. Their love language is rooted in proximity, routine, and a steady emotional presence. They don't need to be the center of attention, just close enough to observe and protect.

Signs of Love from a Protector Cat

- **Staying Nearby Without Demanding Attention**: They'll follow you from room to room or rest at a distance where they can keep watch, often facing outward like a sentry.
- **Positioning themselves strategically**: Sitting between you and the door, watching over sleeping family members, or placing themselves near guests as a quiet buffer.
- **Routine-Based Connection**: Greeting you at the same time each day, sleeping in a designated spot near you, or responding to rituals like bedtime or mealtime with steady presence.
- **Slow, Intentional Contact**: Gentle headbutts, slow blinks, soft vocalizations - all delivered with purpose, not impulse.
- **Heightened Awareness of Your Emotional State:** Subtle shifts in your mood may draw them closer. They may

linger nearby during stressful times or quietly stay within reach when you need them most.

How to Love Them Back

- Maintain routines: Protector cats bond through consistency.
- Respect their need for space: affection is quiet, not clingy.
- Let them keep watch: don't force closeness, allow them to choose their place.
- Speak calmly, move predictably: they respond best to grounded energy.
- Offer secure, designated spaces where they can rest and observe undisturbed.

The Protector's love language is devoted presence. Their affection is not loud; it's intentional and grounded. When they sit near you, follow from a distance, or rest in quiet corners of your home, they're offering a kind of emotional loyalty few other types can match. They don't need to be noticed. They need to know you're safe.

How the Protector Responds to Illness

Sick Behavior:

- Withdraws quietly to hide weakness, often to a dark, private corner.
- May still try to "patrol" or act normal, masking discomfort.
- Eats less, sleeps more, but resists showing vulnerability.

How to Help:

- Respect their privacy but gently check in. Sit nearby, speak softly, and avoid forcing cuddles.
- Keep their environment predictable: same feeding area, same litter placement.
- Use soft vocal tones to reassure ("You're safe; I've got this").
- Watch for subtle declines in grooming or food intake as signs that the "Protector" is running low on strength and needs veterinary care.

Emotional Goal: Let them know you're the Protector now.

Red Flags & Misinterpretations

Protector cats are calm, vigilant, and deeply environment-aware, but their quiet, watchful nature is often misunderstood. What may appear controlling, distant, or anxious is usually an instinctive response to perceived instability, unfamiliar people, or changes in their environment.

Behavior	Often misread as	What it actually signals
Behavior: Sitting in doorways, hallways, or stair landings	Often misread as: Blocking, territorial behavior, or stubbornness	What it actually signals: Perimeter monitoring and a need to track movement through shared spaces
Behavior: Watching guests closely without approaching	Often misread as: Fearfulness, aggression, or antisocial behavior	What it actually signals: Assessing unfamiliar energy and determining whether the environment is safe
Behavior: Withdrawing or hiding during changes in routine	Often misread as: Shyness, sulking, or emotional shutdown	What it actually signals: Overwhelm from environmental instability or too much unpredictability
Behavior:Sitting upright for long periods instead of curling up	Often misread as: Inability to relax or discomfort	What it actually signals: Alert rest; remaining ready to respond while conserving energy
Behavior: Delaying eating or eating lightly until the household settles	Often misread as: Picky eating or loss of appetite	What it actually signals: Vigilance; staying alert while others are active or vulnerable
Behavior: Positioning themselves between you and another person or animal	Often misread as: Possessiveness or dominance	What it actually signals: Protective positioning rooted in loyalty and relationship-based guarding

This chart is designed to meet ADA compliant

Protector cats don't act out; they stand watch. When their environment feels unpredictable or their role as sentinel feels threatened, their behaviors may intensify or turn inward. This is not defiance or withdrawal; it is instinct responding to perceived risk.

If You Live with a Protector

Expect quiet watchfulness, steady routines, and subtle loyalty.

Your cat may position themselves near doors, hallways, or sleeping family members. They may not demand affection, but their presence is deliberate and reassuring.

This is not distance - it's devotion.

This is not control - it's care.

This is protection expressed through calm presence.

Real-Life Story: Sambo

I remember one day when Sambo settled in his usual spot outside the bedroom I shared with my brothers. He sat in the hallway like he was on quiet duty, close enough to track my movements but keeping his space. He watched everything.

A sharp knock hit the front door. I felt my shoulders tense. Sambo rose instantly. He walked toward the sound with that steady, controlled pace he always used when he was assessing something. No noise. No hesitation. He placed himself between me and the door as if it were his job to be there.

I opened the door. A delivery man stood on the step with a package. Sambo shifted just enough to keep both of us in his line of sight. He held his body low and firm, eyes fixed, reading the man with that calm, serious focus he used only in moments that mattered to him. He never acted aggressively. He simply made it clear that he was paying attention.

The delivery man glanced down at him, handed me the box, and stepped back without a word. Sambo stayed alert until the door shut and the footsteps faded.

Only then did he return to his spot outside my room, close enough that I felt the steady weight of his presence. He blinked once, stretched, and settled. He had done his job. He always did.

CHAPTER 4

THE "A" TYPE PERSONALITY - THE ADVENTURER

Style: Adventurer (Expressive, Environment Oriented)

The letter **"A"** stands for **Active, Assertive, Adventurous, Agile, Alert** in these cats.

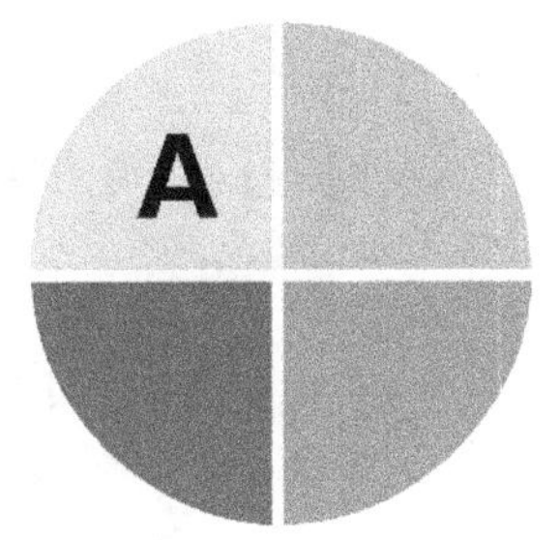

Adventurer cats are bold, high-energy explorers who live for engagement. They're in constant motion, driven by curiosity and a need to interact with the world around them. Every sound is a clue, every open space an invitation. These are the cats climbing shelves, poking their heads into bags, or darting down hallways in spontaneous bursts of play.

Their relationships are built through shared activity. Play for them is recreation and connection. Whether they're batting a toy your way or inviting you into a game of chase, they bond by including you in their world. They express love through action, movement, and proximity during activity, and not by being still.

Without enough stimulation, Adventurers get restless. They don't act out for the sake of mischief, but their energy needs a place to go.

Without it, you'll likely find shredded furniture, sudden bursts of aggression during play, or boundary-pushing behavior. They don't need to be reined in; instead, they just need their energy redirected.

These cats thrive in environments that offer variety, challenge, and give them room to roam. They're happiest when their world is interactive, unpredictable in the right ways, and full of opportunities to lead the adventure.

Primary Motive

To experience, interact, and play. They are not content to simply exist in a space. They need to engage with it.

Instinct in Action: How the Adventurer Engages the World

Adventurer cats experience the world through movement and direct interaction. Their instinct is to engage first and learn through action rather than observation.

An adventurous orange tabby

They respond immediately to novelty like new sounds, objects, smells, or open spaces, by moving toward it, climbing into it, or testing it physically. This is not impulsivity; it is information gathering through experience.

Adventurers explore both horizontally and vertically, using shelves, counters, and high spaces to map their environment. They repeatedly revisit familiar areas to update their understanding as smells and objects change.

Sudden bursts of speed, or "zoomies," serve as energy release and regulation, not chaos.

Because their behavior is active and visible, Adventurers are often misread as mischievous or defiant. In truth, they are communicating something simple:

To know the world, I must engage with it.

When given safe outlets and variety, the Adventurer brings curiosity, momentum, and joy into the home.

Adventurer's Motto: "Life is meant to be explored."

These are the cats who encourage us, sometimes force us, to stay present. Their curiosity invites us to see the world with fresh eyes. They are joy movers, energy shifters, and mood brighteners.

Traits of the Adventurer

Do you have a cat who is constantly hunting mice and birds, then bringing them inside like a treasure? (Leaving blood and guts all over the carpet...) This is a classic adventurer!

Adventurer cats are driven by movement, stimulation, and the thrill of something new. Their behavior is often bold and direct, with an eagerness that can make them seem fearless and, at times, even reckless. They live with intensity and intention, and their actions are fueled by instinct, curiosity, and the desire to engage.

- *High energy and enthusiasm:* These cats rarely sit still. They are quick to react and quick to recover, bouncing from one room to the next or launching into sudden bursts of play. Their energy lifts the mood of a space and keeps things dynamic.
- *Natural curiosity:* Anything new must be explored. Whether it's a crinkling bag, a moving curtain, or a sound outside the window, they need to investigate. Curiosity isn't just a trait; it's how they learn and relate to the world.
- *Confidence:* Adventurers are often unbothered by loud sounds, strangers, or changes in the home. They handle novelty with ease and rarely hesitate when facing something unfamiliar. They are natural leaders among both animals and people.
- *Sociability:* Many Adventurers enjoy interaction, not only with humans but also with other pets. They may initiate play, follow you around the house, or settle near where the action is. Their presence is social and assertive without being needy.
- *Adaptability:* These cats adjust quickly to new environments, schedules, and toys. They tolerate (and often enjoy) change, making them easier to travel with or introduce to new spaces.

Adventurer cats don't wait for the world to come to them. They chase it down. They bring momentum, curiosity, and spark to everyday life and, in doing so, remind us that play, boldness, and presence aren't distractions but how life is fully lived.

Have You Ever Noticed This Behavior?

Have you ever noticed…

…a cat who chooses the open doorway, the high shelf, or the cardboard box over the softest bed in the room? Comfort is available, but curiosity calls louder.

Have you ever noticed…

…a cat who becomes completely absorbed in a sound, shadow, or moving light, ears forward and body locked in focus? In that moment, discovery matters more than everything else.

Have you ever noticed…

…how some cats rotate sleeping spots, rarely choosing the same place twice in a row? Changing locations keeps their world interesting and keeps them alert to what's new.

How Adventurer Cats Bond

Adventurer cats build bonds through activity, not stillness. Their way of connecting is rooted in motion, curiosity, and engagement. They don't seek closeness by curling up in your lap. Instead, they invite you into their world by staying nearby, initiating play, or exploring in your presence.

What Bonding Looks Like for Adventurer Cats

- *They invite you to play*: You'll often see them approach with wide eyes, an upright tail, or a quick paw tap. They may drop a toy at your feet, zoom around you, or initiate a gentle "hunt" sequence. Play is one of their deepest expressions of connection.

- *They include you in their curiosity:* If you're moving from room to room, they'll trail behind or race ahead to investigate first. They may jump onto the counter while you're cooking or insert themselves into your unpacking. To them, shared exploration builds trust.

- *They respond to your voice and attention:* Adventurers often bond through responsive interaction. They'll come when called, follow conversational tone shifts, or vocalize back when spoken to. They engage with presence and alertness.

- *They check in often, even if they don't stay long:* Their version of closeness might be a drive-by rub on your legs, hopping onto a surface near you, or briefly resting beside you before darting off. These are connection moments, not disinterest.

- *They show trust through physical closeness during active states:* Sitting nearby while playing, rolling on their back near you, or napping with one ear tilted your way are all signs of relaxed bonding.

Strengths of the Adventurer

Adventurer cats are more than just active and curious. They bring specific strengths that shape the emotional and energetic rhythm of a household. Their traits make them natural motivators, mood-lifters, and intelligent problem solvers.

- *Joy-bringers:* Adventurers naturally lift the atmosphere wherever they are. Their playfulness, unpredictable antics, and bold spirit remind the people around them not to take life too seriously. Even when their curiosity creates a little chaos, it's hard to stay frustrated because their joy is contagious.

- *Highly intelligent:* These cats are sharp, quick learners who thrive on mental stimulation. They often master routines, open doors, figure out puzzles, or invent their own games. Interactive toys, food mazes, and training sessions challenge them and keep their minds engaged.

- *Resilient and adaptable:* Adventurers recover quickly from setbacks and adjust easily to new experiences. Whether it's a change in environment, a new pet, or a travel situation, they tend to approach it with interest rather than stress. Their ability to stay grounded in movement makes them unusually flexible.

- *Social connectors:* Adventurer cats often act as emotional bridges in the home. They approach people freely, invite play with other pets, and help ease tension in the room. Their outgoing nature fosters interaction and softens social barriers, especially in multi-pet homes or families with young children.

These cats don't just fill space; they energize it. Their strengths don't come from dominance or control, but from presence, curiosity, and their natural gift for inviting connection.

Areas for Growth : When Adventure Becomes Impulse

The same drive that makes Adventurer cats so engaging can also lead them into trouble. Their curiosity, energy, and desire to engage with the world don't come with an off switch, and without clear boundaries or enrichment, their behavior can tip into risk or frustration.

- *Risky behavior:* Adventurers don't always assess danger before acting. They may leap onto hot stovetops, squeeze into vents or cabinets, chew on cords, or dart toward open doors. Though their boldness isn't reckless, it's a boldness driven by a need to explore first and assess later.
- *Overstimulation:* During high-energy play, these cats can become so revved up that they lose awareness of boundaries. What starts as fun pouncing can escalate into swatting, nipping, or biting if they aren't given time to decompress. These behaviors should not be taken for aggression, but intensity without regulation.
- *Restlessness and misbehavior:* When under-stimulated, Adventurers grow bored, and boredom turns into destruction. Scratching furniture, knocking things over, digging in plants, or aggressive zoomies can all be signs of unmet needs for challenge, novelty, or movement.

These cats don't seek chaos, but interaction is their goal. But if that need isn't met intentionally, it can be misread as "bad behavior." Labeling them as hyper or difficult misses the point. What they truly need is structure, stimulation, and outlets for their energy.

Don't Correct This – Support It This Way

Instinct: Explore, investigate, expand territory

Don't correct this…

- Entering every box, bag, or cabinet
- Investigating new smells obsessively
- Testing high or awkward spaces
- Nibbling grass or outdoor plants

Support it this way:

- Rotate safe novelty: boxes, paper bags, scent swaps, puzzle feeders
- Offer vertical exploration (cat trees, shelves)
- Provide cat-safe grass indoors to satisfy tasting instincts
- Let exploration happen before calling them back, then reward engagement

Why it works:

Curiosity fulfilled reduces risky exploration elsewhere.

Adventurer Play Style

Fast, bold, and fully engaged. Adventurer cats play with purpose. For them, play is exploration, problem-solving, and motion. If they're not challenged, they get bored fast, and boredom leads to chaos.

Preferred Toys & Games

- Interactive treat puzzles
  - → Keeps their brain engaged and satisfies their need to "hunt" for rewards.
- Feather wands, laser pointers, motorized prey
  - →These must move quickly and unpredictably. Slow or repetitive movement quickly loses their interest.
- Cat wheels or home agility setups
  - →Perfect for their physical stamina, coordination, and confidence.

- Box mazes, hide-and-seek, exploring new areas
  - →They crave variety. New smells, layouts, and textures keep their senses sharp and their curiosity engaged.

Keep novelty high. Rotate toys weekly and stash them in unexpected spots so they can "rediscover" them. Exploration-based play keeps them mentally stimulated and less likely to create mischief.

How to Create Stability for the Adventurer

Adventurer cats thrive on stimulation, but that doesn't mean they don't need stability. In fact, a reliable, well-managed environment gives them the confidence and freedom to explore safely. The goal isn't to suppress their energy, but to channel it with intention.

Here's how to create the right kind of structure for an Adventurer cat:

1. *Consistent Routines with Flexible Activities*
   - Keep feeding, playtime, and sleeping areas predictable.
   - Add variation within the structure - rotate toys, introduce new objects, or change up play games to prevent boredom without disrupting flow.
2. *Environmental Enrichment*
   - Offer vertical space: cat trees, window shelves, and furniture access.
   - Create "discovery zones" with rotating objects to investigate.
   - Use puzzle feeders or interactive toys to challenge their minds.
3. *Safe Exploration Zones*
   - Give them freedom to roam within secure limits.

- Use barriers, doors, or baby gates to guide movement rather than restrict it entirely.
- If they go outdoors, consider a secure catio or leash training.

4. *Positive Human Interaction*
   - Be part of their world. Talk to them, play with them, and engage when they invite it.
   - Reinforce calm moments, not just high energy ones, to balance their drive.

5. *Recovery Time After Stimulation*
   - Adventurers can crash after bursts of activity. Give them cozy, low-traffic spots where they can rest and self-regulate without disruption.

Adventurer Love Language

Adventurer cats express love by doing, not by holding still. Their love language is rooted in shared activity, curiosity, and physical presence. While they might not be lap cats, they show affection by involving you in their world by inviting you to play, explore, or just be nearby as they stay in motion.

Signs of Love from an Adventurer Cat:

- *Initiating Play:* They drop toys at your feet, bat objects toward you, or do quick zooms around you to invite interaction.
- *Following You Room to Room:* Not because they want to cuddle, but because they want to stay part of whatever you're doing.

- *Physical Proximity Without Pressure:* Sitting next to you while surveying the room, resting nearby during quiet moments, or brushing past your legs mid-adventure.
- *Including You in Exploration*: They'll pause to make eye contact or vocalize during their missions, almost like saying, "Are you seeing this too?"
- *Responsive Interaction*: They chirp back when you talk, respond to their name, or light up when you mirror their energy.

How to Love Them Back:

- Play with them daily. Don't just give toys, be part of the game.
- Talk to them, engage when they invite you in.
- Create safe spaces where they can explore freely.
- Offer novelty and enrichment without overwhelming.
- Respect their pacing. Connection might be quick and intense, not long and cuddly.

The Adventurer's love language is interaction and shared experience. They bond through motion, curiosity, and energy. When they bring you into their playful world, it means they are showing affection in their most natural way.

How the Adventurer Responds to Illness

Sick Behavior:

- Suddenly subdued, lost interest in exploration or play.
- May act frustrated or restless, pacing but not engaging.

- Vocalizes more when uncomfortable, especially if confined.

How to Help:

- Keep their space visually interesting but low effort (window view, gentle background sounds).
- Avoid overstimulation. Quiet, short bursts of affection are better than constant hovering.
- Offer small "choices" to maintain their sense of control: two food bowls, two rest spots.
- Praise minor signs of recovery. A-types respond strongly to positive attention.

Emotional Goal: Protect their spirit of curiosity even when their body can't keep up.

Red Flags & Misinterpretations

Adventurer cats are bold, curious, and driven by exploration, but their high-energy nature is often misunderstood. What appears to be misbehavior is usually a sign of unmet needs or overstimulation, not defiance or aggression.

Here are some common red flags and how they're often misread:

Behavior:	Often misread as:	What it actually signals:
Zooming around the house at night	"Hyper" or attention-seeking	Pent-up energy or lack of stimulation during the day
Knocking objects off shelves	"Being bad" or stubborn	Testing cause-and-effect or seeking interaction
Biting or swatting mid-play	Aggression or meanness	Overstimulation or frustration from repetitive or underwhelming play
Darting out doors or climbing screens	Trying to "escape"	Seeking adventure, stimulation, or environmental enrichment
Pacing or vocalizing when alone	Separation anxiety	Boredom, lack of engagement, or an unmet need for movement

These cats don't act out; they act out of a lack of outlets. When their mental and physical energy isn't channeled, they find their own ways to stay stimulated, which often looks disruptive from a human perspective.

If You Live with an Adventurer

Expect movement, curiosity, engagement, and bursts of intensity. Your cat will explore first, think later, and invite you into their discoveries through play and shared activity.

This is not chaos - it's instinct in motion.

This is not misbehavior - it's curiosity seeking an outlet.

Real-life Story: Maribeth

Maribeth was my Adventurer, and one of the most prominent of my childhood cats. She treated every corner of the house like unexplored territory, but the hall closet was her Everest. One day when I was about 12, she marched up to it, stared at the open door with dramatic purpose, and then, without warning, launched herself inside like a tiny furry missile. My brothers and I turned away from the TV and stared, equally surprised and amused.

There were thumps, scrapes, and one very confident yowl. I wondered, was it a mouse? A large centipede?

When I went over and peeked in, Maribeth was buried halfway behind the shoe rack, digging like she had discovered a secret tunnel. She popped out covered in dust and proudly dropped her "finds" at my feet: a lost glove, then a toy mouse, and finally a charger cable we'd been searching for for months.

She strutted away with the confidence of a cat who had just saved the household.

That was Maribeth, the fearless explorer, chaos specialist, and undefeated champion of closet archaeology.

CHAPTER 5

THE "W" TYPE PERSONALITY – THE WISE ONE

Style: Wise One (Reserved + People-Oriented)

The letter **"W"** stands for **Wise, Watchful, Warm, Withholding, Well-balanced.** Wise One cats bring a quiet intelligence and calm presence to the home. They don't rush into interactions or demand your attention, but observe, reflect, and respond with intention. Their approach to relationships is slow 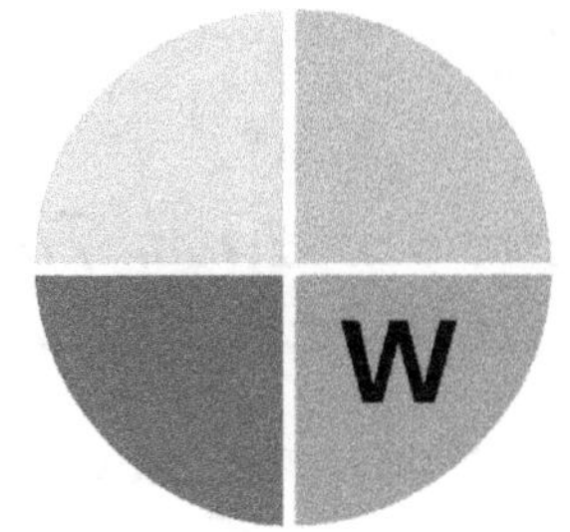 and measured, but once trust is earned, their connection runs deep.

They are drawn to people more than places, yet they're not overtly affectionate. Instead, they choose to stay close in stillness, offering companionship without pressure. These cats are often found resting nearby, quietly witnessing the energy in the room. Their comfort is subtle, but solid.

In homes with tension, grief, or stress, they provide grounding. They're not fixers but stabilizers. Their calm presence can ease anxiety, and their steady energy has a way of anchoring others.

Even other animals tend to give them space and respect, as if sensing their emotional authority.

Wise Ones aren't distant; they're intentional. Their love is expressed in calm presence, quiet company, and emotional steadiness. They don't offer affection freely, but when they do, it feels earned and deeply genuine.

Primary Motive

The Wise One is the quiet center of emotional gravity in the home. This cat doesn't command attention with noise or demand affection with persistence. Instead, they offer something more profound: a steady presence, calm perception, and intuitive emotional balance.

Instinct in Action: How the Wise One Observes and Decides

Our sunroom overlooking the back yard with a wise cat keeping watch. Edited.

Wise One cats move through the world by observing first and engaging selectively. Their instinct is not to rush toward stimulation or insert themselves into activity, but to watch, assess, and choose when interaction is worthwhile. Information is gathered through stillness rather than motion.

One of the most recognizable Wise One behaviors is their tendency to remain at a distance, often in elevated or quiet spaces, where they can see without being seen. This is not avoidance. It is strategic observation. From these vantage points, they monitor changes, patterns, and energy before deciding whether to participate.

Wise One cats conserve energy. They move deliberately, rest in low-traffic areas, and disengage quickly once their need for interaction has been met. When they respond, whether to play, affection, or a call, it is intentional, not automatic. Engagement is a choice, not a reflex.

Because their behaviors are subtle, Wise Ones are often mistaken for aloof or indifferent. In reality, their instinct is precise:

To engage wisely, I must observe first.

When their need for quiet, autonomy, and choice is respected, Wise One cats offer calm presence, thoughtful connection, and steady emotional balance to the home.

Wise One's Motto: "I bring balance where there is noise."

Whether it's household tension, a new pet introduction, or emotional upheaval among humans, the Wise One doesn't react; they respond. Their strength lies in stillness, and through that stillness, they bring harmony.

Traits of the Wise One Type Cat

Wise Ones tend to reveal their personalities through subtle, consistent behavior. They don't command attention with noise or speed. Instead, they influence the environment through calm presence and nonreactive steadiness. These are the cats that seem to carry a quiet knowing in their body language, unhurried, with eyes always alert and reactions measured.

Here's how their temperament typically shows up:

- *Grounded composure:* Wise Ones are rarely startled and rarely frantic. Loud noises, sudden movements, or new visitors might make them pause, but they seldom flee or hide. They hold their space and assess rather than react.

- *Quiet confidence*: These cats don't compete for dominance or attention. They carry a calm self-assurance that makes them feel emotionally untouchable. They don't need to push; they exist with presence.
- *Deep observational intelligence:* Before they act, they observe. A new toy, person, or pet will be quietly studied before any interaction. They read the room better than most humans do.
- *Subtle authority:* In homes with multiple animals, the Wise One often holds an invisible leadership role. Other pets instinctively respect their boundaries. They don't fight for rank, but maintain it through calm consistency.
- *Emotional regulation:* These cats help set the emotional tone. When others are anxious or chaotic, they act as a buffer, modeling calm and often encouraging others to settle just by being nearby.

Wise Ones are often described as "old souls" for a reason. There's something about them that feels experienced and emotionally refined. They're not above the drama and will often choose not to participate in it.

Have You Ever Noticed This Behavior?

Have you ever noticed…

…a cat who watches play from across the room instead of joining in? They aren't left out. They're observing.

Have you ever noticed…

…a cat who prefers high places like stairs, shelves, the back of the couch, where they can see without being in the middle of things? They're gathering information while conserving energy.

Have you ever noticed…

…how some cats pause before responding, even to familiar voices or routines? They aren't slow. They're deciding whether this moment truly requires action.

How a Wise One Bonds

Wise Ones build bonds slowly, quietly, and deliberately. They don't rush into affection or seek constant contact. Instead, they spend time observing, listening, and learning from you. For them, connection is earned through emotional consistency and mutual respect. They pay attention to your energy long before they engage.

When a Wise One begins to bond, it shows in subtle shifts. They'll start sitting closer to you, resting in the same room, or mirroring your emotional state. They may not seek your lap, but they'll lie just nearby, aligning their presence with yours. In their world, closeness is safety, not control.

What Bonding Looks Like in a Wise One

- *Slow proximity:* They begin by watching from a distance. Over time, they inch closer, until they're regularly present in your space without needing interaction.

- *Calm mirroring*: When you're still, they're still. If you're upset, they settle nearby without fuss, creating quiet emotional support.
- *Silent companionship*: They sit beside you, facing outward, showing they're not just with you, but also watching over the space around you.
- *Blinking and soft gaze:* They make unbroken eye contact with soft, slow blinks, which is a deep feline sign of trust.
- *Delayed but deliberate contact*: They may nuzzle your hand or gently brush past your legs, but only when the emotional environment feels right.

Wise Ones don't cling, demand, or hover. Their love is steady and quiet. Bonding with them is less about touching and more about feeling more aligned, moment by moment.

Strengths of the Wise One

Wise Ones offer quiet power. They don't need attention to be effective, and they don't take up space; they simply hold it. Their value in the home is often understated, but once recognized, it becomes clear just how emotionally stabilizing they are. Here's a closer look at what makes them so essential:

- *Emotional Anchoring:*
  - These cats serve as grounding forces. In homes with emotional volatility, whether due to children, grief, illness, or general stress, Wise Ones bring a calm that helps reset the room. They don't absorb the chaos; they neutralize it. Their steady presence has a calming effect on both people and other animals.

- *Silent Leadership:*
  - They don't dominate or control, but their behavior sets the tone. Other pets often follow their lead simply because of the confidence and consistency they carry. They enforce boundaries with their posture, eye contact, and calm authority, rather than with aggression. Ultimately, their leadership is respected and not feared.
- *Mindfulness in Motion:*
  - Everything a Wise One does feels intentional. They move slowly, settle deliberately, and react only when necessary. Their behavior often reminds you to slow down and become more aware and watching them can feel meditative. They embody emotional intelligence in physical form.
- *Low-Maintenance, High-Impact:*
  - Wise Ones rarely demand attention, stimulation, or excessive interaction. They're independent but deeply connected. Without needing much from you, they still provide a strong sense of companionship and comfort. Their influence in the home is often felt more than seen, but it is lasting.

Area for Growth: When Stillness Becomes Withdrawal

The Wise One's quiet presence is often their most defining trait, but that same stillness can sometimes drift into detachment. Because they don't vocalize needs or seek attention the way more expressive cats do, it's easy to miss when they've shifted from calm observation into emotional shutdown.

This risk is mainly present in environments that are too loud, unpredictable, or emotionally heavy. In these situations, Wise Ones may pull away altogether, disappearing into low-traffic areas, avoiding interaction, or sleeping excessively. They do this for self-preservation and not out of stubbornness or moodiness.

Wise Ones tend to withdraw when the following conditions exist:

- *Overstimulating homes:* Constant noise, high energy from other pets, or too much handling can cause them to disengage. When they feel they can't regulate the space, they often remove themselves from it.
- *Emotional neglect:* Because they ask for little, it's easy to forget that they still need moments of connection. When their quiet presence is mistaken for emotional independence, they may begin to feel unseen.
- *Grief or major change:* Loss of a companion, moving homes, or changes in household dynamics can cause Wise Ones to retreat even more deeply into themselves. They process slowly and quietly, and grief can lead to long-term emotional withdrawal if unacknowledged.

You can help the Wise One with gentle, consistent interaction. Let them come to you, but make yourself available. Speak softly. Offer presence rather than pressure and let them know they're seen, not with noise or forced affection, but with time, respect, and patience.

Don't Correct This – Support it This Way

Instinct: Observe, conserve energy, assess before acting

Don't correct this…

- Watching play instead of joining
- Ignoring their name until it truly matters
- Preferring elevated or quiet spaces
- Leaving noisy or chaotic environments

Support it this way:

- Respect choice-based interaction - invite, don't insist
- Create high observation perches with escape routes
- Keep feeding and play routines consistent
- Use gentle cues rather than repeated commands

Why it works:

Wise Ones engage deeply—but only when the moment makes sense.

Play Style

Wise Ones don't chase chaos. Their play style reflects their personality: slow, focused, and purposeful. For them, play isn't about expending energy in wild bursts, but about meaningful interaction, gentle movement, and quiet mental engagement.

They prefer toys and activities that mirror real-world scenarios, like slow-moving prey or thoughtful problem-solving tasks. Too much noise, motion, or stimulation can overwhelm rather than entertain them. They're more likely to walk away from fast-paced games than join in, and when engaged on their terms, however, they reveal a rich inner world of curiosity and quiet delight.

Preferred Toys & Games for Wise Ones

- Wand toys with slow, smooth movement
  - → Gentle swaying or crawling motions mimic real prey and keep them focused without triggering stress. They'll track carefully before striking since timing and control matter more than speed.
- Low-level treat puzzles or foraging mats
  - → Simple puzzles provide quiet mental stimulation. They enjoy the calm, steady reward of solving something rather than racing for a prize.
- Laser pointers (slow and controlled)
  - → When used at a slower pace and with an eventual reward (like a treat or toy catch), laser play can satisfy their need for movement without overstimulation.
- Minimalist textured toys (felt, rope, soft crinkle)
  - → Tactile feedback is soothing for Wise Ones. They prefer grounded materials and subtle interaction to flashy or erratic toys.

Creating Stability for the Wise One

Wise Ones thrive in spaces where the energy is predictable and the environment feels emotionally balanced. They don't just react to what's happening around them; they absorb it. So, the more consistent and calm the home, the safer they feel. If routines shift too often or emotions run high, they're likely to retreat and become disconnected.

You can help Wise Ones with a structured environment:

- *Predictable routines:* Stick to consistent feeding times, quiet resting hours, and stable daily patterns. Surprises, especially loud or rushed ones, can throw them off emotionally.
- *Emotionally safe environments:* Tone matters. Yelling, sudden outbursts, or even tense arguments can make them withdraw. A calm voice, slow movements, and respectful energy encourage them to stay emotionally present.
- *Low-stimulation resting spaces:* Give them access to quiet, out-of-the-way spots where they can observe without being disturbed, like high perches, soft corners, or covered beds. These become their emotional reset zones.
- *Clear, gentle engagement:* Invite interaction calmly. They don't want to be grabbed or pursued. Wait for their signal. Speak softly, blink slowly, and let them come to you.
- *Protect boundaries from other pets or guests:* They dislike chaos, especially from more dominant or high-energy animals. Intervene if their space is being invaded, and don't force them to socialize on demand.

Wise Ones don't need perfect conditions, but they do need predictability. Stability allows them to stay open, present, and emotionally connected.

The Wise One's love language

Wise Ones express love through stillness and proximity, not touch or attention-seeking. Their version of closeness is subtle but deeply intentional. They don't smother, demand, or chase affection. Instead, they choose to be with you: nearby, alert, and calm. Their love isn't loud; It's felt.

Signs of Love from a Wise One

- Being in the same room, without needing attention: They follow you, not to interact, but to share the space. Presence = trust.
- Slow blinking: One of the clearest signals of affection and comfort. It means: *I trust you. I feel safe.*
- Watching you calmly from a distance: If they're perched somewhere nearby with a soft gaze, they're not just observing; they're connected.
- Sitting beside you, facing outward: A subtle protective gesture. They're "with" you while keeping watch over the space.
- Quiet vocalizations (rare but soft): A light chirp or hum may come when you enter the room or during calm one-on-one time. It's their version of saying hello.
- Grooming near you: Grooming in your presence signals relaxation and trust. Sometimes, they'll even groom themselves while resting beside you, content and at ease.
- Choosing you in moments of stress: If you're having a hard day and they settle nearby without fuss, that's their way of saying, *I'm here for you.*

How to Love the Wise One Back

To love a Wise One is to honor the quiet. They don't need grand gestures or constant engagement. What they value most is emotional steadiness, predictable rhythms, and a space where they can observe, rest, and connect on their terms.

Ways to Show Love to a Wise One

- Respect their silence: Don't push affection or interrupt their stillness. Sit nearby. Let them make the first move. Be with them, not on them.
- Create emotional consistency: Speak gently. Keep your tone even. Avoid shouting, slamming, or chaos. They feel energy shifts even if they don't respond visibly.
- Build routines: Feed, play, and rest around the exact times each day. They feel more secure when the world around them is predictable.
- Offer quiet engagement: Use slow blinks, soft speech, or stillness as ways to connect. Let eye contact and presence be the bond.
- Protect their boundaries: Intervene if other pets or people overstep their space. They won't defend themselves loudly, but they will silently retreat if overwhelmed.
- Acknowledge their support: They may not climb into your lap when you're upset, but their presence beside you is deliberate. Recognize it for what it is: care.

How the Wise One Responds to Illness

Sick Behavior:

- Withdraws into deep stillness, less movement, long stares, and less blinking.
- Often misread as "just sleeping more."
- May hide symptoms until late stages.

How to Help:

- Monitor carefully and take any change seriously. Wise Ones hide pain masterfully.
- Keep energy in the room calm; they dislike chaos during vulnerability.
- Speak softly and use a consistent touch if they allow it.
- Use familiar scents (like your blanket or a favorite toy) to anchor them.

Emotional Goal: Create a sanctuary of peace, not pity, where they can heal without fear.

Red Flags & Misinterpretations

Wise One cats are observant, discerning, and highly selective in how they engage with the world. Their quiet independence and measured responses are often misunderstood. What may appear distant or indifferent is usually a thoughtful assessment of safety, value, and energy.

Behavior	Often misread as	What it actually signals
Watching from a distance without approaching	Aloofness or lack of attachment	Thoughtful observation and a preference for understanding before engaging
Choosing solitude over social interaction	Disinterest or rejection	Selective energy use and a need for mental and emotional autonomy
Delayed or minimal response to calls or commands	Stubbornness or defiance	Discernment - responding only when the interaction feels meaningful or necessary
Frequently changing resting spots to quiet, elevated areas	Avoidance or anxiety	A need for low-stimulation environments and strategic observation points
Limited tolerance for handling or forced affection	Coldness or lack of affection	Strong boundaries and a preference for consent-based connection
Sudden withdrawal after brief interaction	Moodiness or unpredictability	Mental saturation - needing space to process stimulation

Wise One cats don't disengage because they don't care; they disengage because they are choosing carefully. Their calm presence is rooted in discernment, not detachment. When respected, they form deep, quiet bonds built on mutual trust.

If You Live with a Wise One

Expect observation, independence, and quiet discernment.

Your cat may watch more than they act, choose solitude over stimulation, and engage on their own terms. Their trust is slow to earn and deeply intentional.

This is not aloofness - it's wisdom.

This is not disinterest - it's selective connection.

Real-Life Story: Jacko

Jacko was the most distinctive Wise One in my childhood. He was calm, thoughtful, and quietly convinced he was the emotional supervisor of the entire household. One day I recall as a teen, several other cats were having a full-blown meltdown or spat over absolutely something or nothing. This wasn't that unusual mind you, with so many cats coming and going. It could have been someone walked too close to the food bowl, someone else looked suspicious, etc., and suddenly it was chaos.

I recall being about to intervene when Jacko appeared at the doorway like a monk arriving at a protest.

He didn't hiss.
He didn't growl.
He didn't even blink.

He walked into the center of the room, turned in a perfect slow circle, and sat down, facing outward like a furry lighthouse scanning for nonsense.

Instantly, the other cats froze.
Maribeth stopped mid-drama.
Even the food-bowl offender retreated.

Jacko looked at them with his classic expression of:

"This is beneath all of you. Please compose yourselves."

Within seconds, the room went silent.

Crisis ended.

Peace restored.

Jacko didn't move; he just flicked his tail once like he had personally saved civilization.

That was Jacko, a quiet authority, zero chaos, and the only cat I know who could stop an argument simply by existing. Scenes like that have stayed with me to this day.

THE "S" TYPE PERSONALITY – THE SENSITIVE SOUL

Style: Sensitive Soul (Expressive + People-Oriented)

The letter "S" stands for Sensitive, Soft, Sweet, Supportive, and Sincere in these cats. Sensitive Soul cats are emotional mirrors. Their empathy runs deep, and they absorb the emotional atmosphere around them. Whether it's joy, sadness, or stress, they pick it up quickly and often respond with quiet gestures of connection. They might approach gently when you're upset, blink slowly to show affection, or curl against your side when words aren't enough.

They bond deeply with their humans and thrive on mutual emotional closeness. Their affection isn't random but intentional and often responsive to your mood. You'll hear soft meows, feel warm nudges, or notice them staring with soft, unblinking eyes. These cats are expressive in subtle, intuitive ways.

But their emotional openness also makes them vulnerable. Loud environments, tension, or unpredictable changes can easily overwhelm them. They benefit most from stable, gentle homes where their sensitivity is respected rather than corrected.

Sensitive Souls are affectionate and emotionally invested. They don't just want your presence; instead, they want to feel connected to it.

Primary Motive

The Sensitive Soul is the empath of the feline world, a quiet, intuitive companion whose heart beats in rhythm with the emotional pulse of their home. These cats don't simply notice your moods; they absorb them. When you're anxious, they become watchful, and when you're sad, they soften beside you. Their affection is quiet but profound, an emotional presence that comforts without words.

Instinct in Action: How the Sensitive Soul Responds to the World

Sensitive Soul cats experience the world through heightened awareness of sound, movement, and emotional shifts. Their instinct is not to control or explore, but to *sense* and respond. Information is gathered through subtle cues rather than direct action.

My wife in our sunroom with a sensitive cat

They react quickly to changes in tone, routine, or environment, often retreating when stimulation feels too intense. This withdrawal is not fear or weakness; it is self-regulation. By creating distance, the Sensitive Soul protects their nervous system.

These cats often seek gentle proximity like sitting close, touching lightly, or following quietly, especially when emotions in the home shift. Connection helps them regulate, while chaos overwhelms.

Because their responses are emotional and internal, Sensitive Souls are often misread as fragile or needy. In truth, they are communicating something simple:

I feel everything.

When their environment is calm and predictable, Sensitive Soul cats offer deep attunement, empathy, and quiet affection.

Sensitive Soul's Motto: "I feel what you feel."

Whether it's curling up beside you when you cry, nuzzling your face after an argument, or becoming withdrawn when you're overwhelmed, the Sensitive Soul reflects the emotional tone of the household with uncanny precision. They don't require words. They read energy.

Traits of a Sensitive Soul Cat

My wife's family cat growing up, Mysti, a beautiful blue point Siamese, was a classic sensitive soul. Whenever Mysti heard my wife (or any of her siblings) crying, she would rush over, snuggle in, and try to comfort.

My wife's family cat growing up, Mysti, a beautiful blue point Siamese, was a classic sensitive soul. Whenever Mysti heard my wife (or any of her siblings) crying, she would rush over, snuggle in, and try to comfort.

Sensitive Souls move through the world with a kind of quiet grace: soft in presence, but deep in feeling. Their emotional radar is finely tuned, and they seem to feel before they think. Every gesture, glance, or tone of voice reaches them in ways we often underestimate. To live with a Sensitive Soul is to share space with a creature who reflects your inner weather, sometimes mirroring it, and sometimes balancing it.

Sensitive Souls are known for:

- Emotional Intuition: These cats can sense shifts in mood the way others sense temperature. They notice subtle cues, such as changes in breathing, body posture, or energy, and adapt accordingly. When you're sad, they may quietly settle beside you; when you're calm, they stretch and relax as if the air itself has softened. Their empathy is silent but unmistakable.

- Gentle Affection: Their love language is tenderness, a soft paw on your hand, a slow purr pressed against your chest, a light grooming of your hair or fingers. They express closeness through physical gentleness rather than exuberance. You rarely need to call them because they arrive when you need them most.

- Cautious Behavior: Sensitive Souls are easily startled by raised voices, sudden movements, or harsh environments. They thrive on consistency and emotional safety. To them, tone means more than words; they read it like a script. A loud sound or impatient gesture can send them retreating, not from defiance, but from self-protection.

- Strong Individual Bonds: These cats choose their people with care. While polite to others, they often form one deep, devoted attachment, a soul-level connection that feels almost telepathic. Once bonded, they are unwavering in loyalty and can even experience separation stress if their person is away too long.

- Need for Calm and Predictability: In chaotic or noisy environments, Sensitive Souls may withdraw, hide, or seem aloof. This isn't rejection; it's regulation. They need peaceful spaces where their delicate emotional equilibrium can reset. Gentle routines, soft voices, and stable energy allow them to blossom into the affectionate, trusting companions they're meant to be.

To strangers, a Sensitive Soul may seem shy or detached. But to the person they trust, they reveal a world of quiet devotion, a steady, intuitive love that hums just beneath the surface. These cats remind us that strength doesn't always roar; sometimes, it simply purrs.

Have You Ever Noticed This Behavior?

Have you ever noticed…

…a cat who nibbles grass, chews on plants, or seeks out textures after a stressful moment? It's not misbehavior; it's self-soothing.

Have you ever noticed…

…a cat who turns their head away, slow blinks, yawns, or licks their lips when things feel intense? They're signaling a need for calm, not disengaging.

Have you ever noticed…

…how some cats press close to you, curl tightly, or retreat into small, enclosed spaces when overwhelmed? Gentle pressure and containment bring safety.

How a Sensitive Soul Bonds

Bonding with a Sensitive Soul isn't an event but an unfolding. These cats don't rush into affection; they build it slowly, through mutual safety and consistency. For them, trust is sacred currency, and every interaction is a small emotional transaction that either strengthens or weakens that trust.

Sensitive Souls bond not through big gestures, but through presence. This is the most valid form of connection for them: not constant touch, but constant attunement.

Their Bonding Blueprint

- Safety Before Affection: Before they give affection, they need to feel emotionally and physically safe. A calm voice, gentle eye contact, and predictable movements speak louder than petting or play. Once safety is established, affection flows naturally and deeply.
- Silent Observation: Sensitive Souls often "watch before they join." When they first enter a space or relationship, they study the energy, learning who moves fast, who stays grounded, and where peace lives. Observation is their way of saying, I'm getting to know you.
- Gradual Approach: They bond in stages: presence → proximity → touch → trust. Rushing this process can break the flow; honoring it builds an unshakable bond.
- Reciprocal Energy: These cats are emotional mirrors. When you're patient and gentle, they reflect calm curiosity. When you're tense, they absorb that tension. Their bond deepens when they feel your energy is safe to inhabit.

- Deep One-to-One Connection: Once bonded, a Sensitive Soul often chooses "their person", the human whose energy feels most aligned. That connection becomes profound and enduring, sometimes lasting a lifetime. They may greet that person with eye contact, quiet vocalizations, or simply by following them from room to room.

What Bonding Looks Like

To the untrained eye, bonding from a Sensitive Soul might look understated, but to those who know them, it's a language of subtle devotion.

You'll know you're bonded when:

- They choose to be near you, sitting just close enough to share space without demanding attention.
- They make soft, prolonged eye contact, often followed by a slow blink, which is their version of "I love you."
- They bring you small tokens (a toy, a leaf, a piece of lint) as offerings of trust.
- They touch gently, a paw on your hand, a nose against your cheek, and wait for your response.
- They begin to match your daily rhythm, resting when you rest, appearing when you need quiet company.
- In times of distress, they may rest near your heart or curl by your side, not seeking comfort, but offering it.

Bonding with a Sensitive Soul feels less like ownership and more like a shared spiritual agreement, which says: *I will protect your peace, and you will defend mine.*

Strengths of the Sensitive Soul

The Sensitive Soul may not command a room, but they change its atmosphere simply by being in it. Their power is subtle, their gifts quiet, but those who live with them know their presence transforms a home. These cats remind us that gentleness and strength are not opposites, but partners.

Key Strengths

Emotional Intelligence: Sensitive Souls are masters of empathy. They sense emotional undercurrents long before words or actions reveal them. Whether it's curling beside you after a stressful day or purring softly during grief, they know what you need on an intuitive level. Their ability to absorb and mirror emotion is a rare form of intelligence, one that heals as much as it connects.

Deep Loyalty: Once a Sensitive Soul has chosen you, their bond is unshakable. They remain near you through every season, not out of dependence, but devotion. They don't offer love to everyone, which makes their trust sacred. When a Sensitive Soul lets you in, it's for keeps.

Calming Presence: Their energy soothes both humans and other animals. Sensitive Souls bring emotional balance to the spaces they inhabit by lowering tension, softening conflict, and creating an atmosphere of peace. Their stillness is their strength, and their quiet company often provides comfort when words cannot.

Thoughtful Observation: Before acting, these cats observe. This patience allows them to learn routines, anticipate changes, and adapt gracefully. They rarely overreact; instead, they study their environment until it feels safe. That reflective nature makes them sensitive and intelligent.

Authentic Affection: They love without pretense or performance. Their affection isn't about attention but about connection. When they choose to sit beside you, it's genuine. Every blink, every soft paw, every gentle nuzzle is intentional, full of meaning. Their love is quiet, but it's absolute.

Emotional Healing: Sensitive Souls have a near-magical ability to absorb human emotion and return calm. Many caretakers describe them as "therapists with fur." Their sensitivity makes them natural healers because they sense where tension lives and settle near it until the energy shifts.

In essence, the Sensitive Soul's greatest strength is their capacity to feel deeply without judgment. They remind us that gentleness is not weakness, and sensitivity is not fragility; it is wisdom expressed through empathy. Their presence invites us to slow down, listen closely, and love with greater awareness.

Area for Growth: When Empathy Becomes Overload

For the Sensitive Soul, empathy is both a gift and a weight. Their emotional radar runs so high that what soothes others can sometimes overwhelm them. They don't just notice energy; they absorb it. And without boundaries, that deep attunement can turn into emotional exhaustion.

These cats feel the world in full color: every sound, movement, and emotion vibrates through them. While this sensitivity makes them extraordinary companions and healers, it also makes them vulnerable to overstimulation, stress, and imbalance.

When empathy becomes overload, the Sensitive Soul may:

- Retreat or hide during arguments, raised voices, or household tension, not out of fear, but as an act of emotional self-preservation.
- Develop stress-related behaviors such as over-grooming, appetite loss, digestive issues, or restless pacing in chaotic or unstable environments.
- Withdraw from interaction when exposed to too many people, other pets, or sudden changes. Even positive excitement (guests, holidays, new furniture) can feel overwhelming.
- Mirror human distress so deeply that they appear "sick" when their person is emotionally depleted, reflecting the energy they've absorbed.

Their nervous systems are finely tuned instruments: beautiful, responsive, and delicate. When the environment hums with calm, they thrive. But when it buzzes with tension, their balance falters.

Don't Correct This – Support It This Way

Instinct: Regulate nervous system, maintain emotional harmony

Don't correct this…

- Hiding during loud or emotional moments
- Kneading, fabric sucking, or pressing into tight spaces
- Over-grooming after stress
- Sitting nearby without seeking touch

Support it this way:

- Provide safe retreat spaces (covered beds, closets, boxes)
- Use soft textures and familiar scents
- Keep voices and movements gentle during stress
- Let proximity be enough; don't demand interaction

Why it works:

Regulation comes before connection.

Play Style

Play is about emotional bonding and stress relief. Sensitive Souls prefer soft, non-threatening engagement and can be easily over-stimulated.

Preferred Toys & Games:

- Soft plush toys
    - → Ideal for gentle wrestling, kneading, or comfort-carrying
- Feather teasers or gentle wand toys
    - → Used at a slow pace to invite rather than challenge
- Interactive toys that they can control (like toys that squeak or move slightly)
    - → Helps reduce anxiety and builds confidence
- Small, crinkly toys or calming scent-infused items (lavender, catnip, silvervine)
    - → Appeals to their sensory side without overstimulation

How to Create Stability for a Sensitive Soul

For the Sensitive Soul, stability is more than comfort; it's survival. Their emotional world depends on predictability, peace, and gentle rhythm. When the energy around them is steady, their natural empathy becomes a strength. When it's chaotic, it becomes overwhelming.

Creating stability means providing an environment, both physical and emotional, that tells them: You're safe here. The world is kind.

Keep a Steady Routine

Routine is the Sensitive Soul's anchor. Regular feeding times, play sessions, and quiet hours help them feel the world is reliable. Even minor disruptions like a late meal or a sudden visitor can ripple through their nervous system. Keep change slow, intentional, and transparent. For example:

- Introduce new foods gradually by mixing them with the familiar.
- Announce vet trips gently; bring out the carrier early and reward calm exploration.
- Return furniture or litter boxes to the same spot after cleaning; predictability equals safety.

Manage the Emotional Climate

These cats live attuned to your tone, pace, and energy. They don't just inhabit your home; they absorb its atmosphere.

To create emotional steadiness:

- Speak softly, even during correction or excitement.
- Move calmly; sudden gestures can be misread as threats.
- Use background calmers such as low music, soft white noise, or nature sounds.
- If tension arises (arguments, loud television, energetic gatherings), create a quiet retreat space for them, a sanctuary where energy stays neutral.

Your calm is their compass. When you ground yourself, they find theirs.

Provide a Safe Retreat

Every Sensitive Soul needs a "peace zone", a place where they can retreat without being followed or called. This can be:

- A cozy covered bed tucked into a corner.
- A perch near a window but away from foot traffic.
- A soft carrier left open and always available.

This space should always smell familiar and remain untouched during stress or illness. Over time, it becomes their emotional recharge station.

Encourage Gentle Confidence

Too much protection can make a Sensitive Soul timid. Stability doesn't mean stagnation; it means safe growth.

- Introduce new experiences slowly, one sense at a time.

- Celebrate small acts of bravery, like exploring a new toy or approaching a new visitor.
- Use calm praise and gentle touch as affirmation, never pressure.

Confidence for them grows not from exposure, but from choice when they feel free to approach the unknown on their terms, and courage blooms.

Stay Emotionally Transparent

They read your moods better than you do. If you're upset, it's okay. Acknowledge it calmly. Pretending everything's fine while radiating tension only confuses them. Speak softly and honestly:

"I'm okay, I'm just having a hard day."

Your voice steadies them more than your silence ever could.

Restore Energy Balance

After stress, like a vet visit, travel, houseguests, plan a "recovery window." Lower noise, simplify space, and reestablish routine. Let your cat dictate the pace of reconnection. Stability is rebuilt through rhythm, not rush.

The Gift of Stability

When a Sensitive Soul feels secure, they bloom. Their empathy deepens, their playfulness returns, and their affection becomes radiant. In stability, their intuition turns into insight as they begin to feel their emotions and balance them.

Creating stability isn't about controlling the world around them; it's about cultivating peace within it. In that peace, the Sensitive Soul reveals their most authentic self: calm, loving, and luminous.

Sensitive Soul's Love Language

The Sensitive Soul doesn't shout their affection; they breathe it. Their love language is built on presence, empathy, and gentle energy. They bond not through what you do, but how you are around them. To a Sensitive Soul, love means safety, softness, and consistency, the kind of love that doesn't need to be loud to be felt.

They fall in love with the calm in your voice, the predictability of your touch, and the peace that radiates from your stillness.

When they love you, they match your rhythm, absorb your moods, and wrap their quiet heart around yours.

Signs of Love from a Sensitive Soul

To the untrained eye, these gestures may seem small, but they are declarations of devotion spoken in feline poetry.

- Silent Companionship: They sit near you without demanding attention, often facing the same direction as if sharing your thoughts.
- Soft Eye Contact and Slow Blinks: Their gaze lingers, unguarded and steady, followed by the unmistakable slow blink of trust and love.
- Subtle Mirroring: You sigh, they stretch. You settle, they settle. They unconsciously attune their body language and energy to yours.

- Heart-Centered Touch: They may place a paw on your chest or rest near your heart, purring softly, to sync with your emotional core.
- Protective Proximity: They follow you from room to room, not out of neediness but from a quiet wish to keep their chosen human within emotional sight.
- Vulnerability: They show their belly not for play but as the ultimate act of trust, which says: "I am unguarded with you."

To them, love is peaceful attention. When they are with you in stillness, they are saying, "This is my heart, and you are safe in it".

How to Love a Sensitive Soul Back

Loving a Sensitive Soul means meeting them where they live, in quiet awareness. They don't need grand gestures; they need gentleness that feels genuine.

- *Speak the Language of Calm:* Keep your movements fluid and your voice steady. Your tone means more than your words. Even a soft "hello" carries emotional weight when spoken with warmth.
- *Offer Predictable Affection:* Approach on their terms, not yours. Let them initiate touch, and respond with slow, deliberate pets. Predictable affection builds trust; impulsive affection can startle.
- *Be Emotionally Honest:* They sense incongruence. If you're upset, they'll know. You don't need to fake calmness, but show emotional steadiness. Please take a deep breath before engaging; it tells them your energy is safe to enter.

- *Validate Their Sensitivity:* Never mock or dismiss their cautiousness. Their awareness is not fragility; it's wisdom. Speak to them as you would to a friend who feels deeply, with patience and empathy.
- *Reassure Through Routine:* Rituals of affection like morning greetings, evening cuddles, and bedtime rituals anchor their hearts. Repetition equals reassurance.
- *Protect Their Peace:* Be their emotional filter. When life grows noisy or tense, offer them a stable center like dim lights, soft music, and slow breathing. Your serenity is their shelter.

How the Sensitive Soul Responds to Illness

Sick Behavior:

- Clings or cries more than usual; seeks reassurance through proximity.
- May lose appetite or develop stress-related symptoms.
- Overreacts to medical routines (pills, carriers, vet visits).

How to Help:

- Keep them physically close. A cozy bed near your workspace often helps.
- Use gentle routines before treatments (soothing voice, soft towel).
- Avoid abrupt noises or handling changes; emotional calm speeds their recovery.
- Lavender-scented diffusers or soft instrumental music can help them relax (if safe for cats).

Emotional Goal: Remind them they're not alone; your calm presence is medicine.

Red Flags and Misinterpretations

Sensitive Soul cats are emotionally attuned, deeply responsive, and highly affected by their environment. Their heightened awareness often makes them appear fragile or needy, but their behavior is rooted in perception, not weakness.

Sensitive Soul cats don't overreact; they feel deeply. Their behaviors are signals of emotional processing, not manipulation or fragility. When their environment is gentle and predictable, their sensitivity becomes empathy, affection, and profound connection.

Behavior	Often misread as	What it actually signals
Hiding or retreating during loud noise or chaos	Fearfulness or poor socialization	Sensory overload and a need for emotional safety
Clinging closely or following persistently	Neediness or separation anxiety	Seeking regulation through proximity and reassurance
Startling easily or reacting strongly to sudden changes	Overreaction or nervous temperament	A finely tuned nervous system responding to subtle shifts
Changes in appetite or grooming during stress	Illness or stubborn behavior	Emotional distress affecting physical regulation
Vocalizing softly or frequently when unsettled	Attention-seeking	Communicating discomfort or seeking reassurance
Withdrawing after negative interactions	Holding a grudge or sulking	Self-protection and emotional recovery

If You Live with A Sensitive Soul

Expect emotional attunement, gentleness, and deep responsiveness.

Your cat may mirror your moods, seek reassurance during stress, and retreat quickly when overwhelmed. Their nervous system is finely tuned to their environment.

This is not fragility - it's sensitivity.

This is not neediness - it's emotional awareness.

Real-life Story: Molly

Molly was my most distinct Sensitive Soul. She was soft-hearted, tender, and tuned into human emotions like a tiny furry therapist. But one day, she demonstrated just how *deeply* she felt... and how dramatically she reacted.

I was trying to open a stubborn jar in the kitchen. After ten or so failed attempts, I muttered, "Oh come on!" not yelling, not angry, just mildly annoyed.

Molly, however, heard this as a full emotional crisis.

From across the room, her head popped up like a startled meerkat. Her eyes went wide. She made a tiny, heartbroken "mrrrp?" and rushed over, tail tucked like she was approaching someone on the brink of disaster.

Then she did the most Molly thing possible.

She gently placed one paw on my foot.

Just one.

Very slowly.

As if grounding me in a moment of spiritual healing.

I froze. She froze. We stared at each other in utter seriousness... while I still held a jar of sardines (it's a Caribbean thing).

I told her, "I'm okay, Molly, I'm just frustrated."

She blinked at me once, long, slow, and painfully earnest, then settled against my ankle like she was administering emotional CPR.

For the rest of the night, she followed me around the house with worried eyes, occasionally checking in with another soft "mrrp?" as if making sure I hadn't spiraled into hopeless despair over the jar.

That was Molly: tender, devoted, deeply attuned…and absolutely convinced that every minor inconvenience was an emotional emergency, she had to personally fix.

A SMALL FAVOR
FROM THE AUTHOR

You've now met all four P.A.W.S. personality types: the Protector, the Adventurer, the Wise One, and the Sensitive Soul. By this point, many readers recognize their cat clearly… and often see parts of themselves reflected as well.

If this framework has helped you better understand your cat's behavior, respond with more empathy, or feel more connected to the relationship you share, I'd truly appreciate you taking a moment to leave a review. Attach a picture of your furry feline friend too!

Your review doesn't need to be long or formal. A few honest sentences about what resonated with you, which P.A.W.S. type stood out most, or how this book shifted your perspective can make a meaningful difference. Reviews help other readers decide if this book is right for them, and help this work reach the people and pets who may benefit from it.

Thank you for reading this far, for reflecting deeply, and for being part of the P.A.W.S. community.

Now, let's continue turning insight into a deeper connection.

With gratitude,

- J.W. Kincaid

CHAPTER 7

BLENDED TRAITS

WHEN YOUR CAT IS
MORE THAN ONE TYPE

Just as no two humans are identical in temperament, no two cats fit perfectly inside one box, even a loving one. The **P.A.W.S. Framework** is a map, not a label. It helps us recognize patterns of motivation and emotional behavior, but those patterns are as fluid and nuanced as the cats themselves. While most cats express one dominant type: Protector (P), Adventurer (A), Wise One (W), or Sensitive Soul (S), it's common for them to exhibit blended traits that overlap or shift depending on environment, life stage, and emotional state.

Understanding your cat's blend is about redefining and recognizing the dynamic nature of personality. Your cat may lead with one type but borrow strengths from another. That blend tells a deeper story about who they are, not just how they behave, but how they adapt.

Why Cats Rarely Fit Just One Type

Unlike human personality models that rely on self-assessment, the **P.A.W.S. Framework** is observational. It reflects behavior shaped by instinct, experience, and environment, all living systems in motion.

A kitten who grows up in a calm home may be Sensitive, but if introduced to a confident feline mentor, Adventurer traits can emerge. A Wise One who's lost trust may take on Protector instincts for survival.

In short, your cat's personality evolves with context, not contradiction. Blended traits are a sign of emotional intelligence and adaptability, not inconsistency.

The Core Blends

Just as colors merge where they meet, personality types flow into one another, creating an infinite range of temperaments. No cat is one pure note; they are symphonies, layers of instinct, experience, and emotional learning that blend into a distinctive melody.

When we understand blended traits, we stop expecting our cats to behave in predictable, linear ways. Instead, we begin to see the continuum of their emotional world, as curiosity can coexist with caution, independence can merge with empathy, and confidence can live beside tenderness.

These blended personalities aren't contradictions, but integrations, the living proof that cats, like people, evolve through relationships and their environment.

Why Blends Form

Blends develop for several natural reasons:

1. *Environment and Upbringing:* A kitten raised in a calm, structured home might develop Protector qualities, while one raised with stimulating enrichment might lean

Adventurer, and a cat who experiences both safety and exploration can embody both energies.

2. *Life Experience:* Trauma, trust, recovery, or bonded companionship can permanently shift a cat's personality balance. A once-cautious Wise One may soften into a Sensitive Soul through love and predictability. A Sensitive Soul who learns confidence may grow into a Gentle Protector (S/P), emotionally intuitive yet courageous.

3. *Social Dynamics:* In multi-cat homes, personality balance often forms through complementary adaptation. If one cat plays the Protector role, another may evolve into a Sensitive or Wise role to maintain harmony. Blends can therefore emerge as a social language rather than just an individual trait.

4. *Emotional Maturity:* Just like people, cats mature emotionally over time. A youthful Adventurer may later integrate the reflection of a Wise One, or a Protector may grow softer and more empathetic with age. These blends represent growth, not inconsistency.

🐾 Real Life Example of a Blended Cat: Rhu

Photograph of Rhu from Christmas 2022

Rhubie, to whom this book is dedicated, lived in several foreign countries and across two continents, making her truly my wife's blended cat. In her younger years, Rhu embodied the **Adventurer** - curious, confident, and eager to explore each new environment. As she grew older and her pace naturally slowed, her personality gently evolved. Her primary traits shifted toward those of the **Sensitive Soul** and the **Wise One**. She became deeply intuitive and emotionally attuned to my stepson when she went to live with him in Canada. She offered quiet comfort, calm presence, and reflection rather than motion.

Sadly Rhubie passed away in 2024, but her life beautifully illustrates how blended traits form through experience, environment, and emotional maturity. She reminds us that personality is not static, but is shaped by love, safety, and time.

What Blends Reveal

Blended personalities reveal a cat's emotional intelligence and resilience. They show that your cat is not reacting, but responding, adapting, and integrating past experiences into a balanced way of being. Each combination expresses a unique emotional architecture:

- A balance of instinct and curiosity (P/A).
- A union of reflection and empathy (W/S).
- A synthesis of sensitivity and courage (S/P).

When you identify your cat's blend, you uncover the story behind their behavior, a narrative of how they learned to trust, play, and express love in their own language.

How to Read a Blend

Think of blended types as dual lenses:

- The first type reveals your cat's *primary drive* - the "why" behind their actions.
- The second type expresses their *approach* - the "how" of their behavior.

For instance:

- A Protector/Adventurer acts from a need for safety (Protector) but expresses it through exploration (Adventurer).
- A Wise/Sensitive cat seeks understanding (Wise) and communicates it through empathy (Sensitive).

Blends, therefore, give you two keys: one to motivation, and one to expression. When you learn both, you don't just decode what your cat does; you understand who they are becoming.

Why Blended Cats Are Emotionally Advanced

Blended cats are emotionally bilingual. They can "speak" in two dialects of the **P.A.W.S. Framework**. For example, using Protector logic in times of change and Sensitive empathy in times of calm.

They adjust more fluidly to new environments, comfort others with greater precision, and often act as peacekeepers in multi-pet homes. In short, blends represent the evolution of temperament: the point where instinct meets awareness.

Below are the most common combinations and what they reveal.

Protector - Adventurer (P/A): The Confident Leader

Core Drive: To keep order through exploration and control.

These cats are assertive yet curious. They are bold enough to engage, structured enough to lead. They patrol their world with purpose, confident in their territory but drawn to novelty.

You'll see:

- They approach strangers first but stay alert for changes in tone or energy.
- They're playful but prefer to initiate; they like to set the terms.
- They may correct other pets with a soft swat, not to be aggressive, but for governance.

Balance: Give them space to lead, but also teach them rest. Predictable play and clear boundaries help them channel leadership into trust, and not tension.

Adventurer - Wise One (A/W): The Curious Philosopher

Core Drive: To understand through experience.

These cats are both thinkers and explorers. They observe before pouncing, study before deciding, and thrive on discovery that feels safe.

You'll see:

- They'll test new toys methodically before diving in.
- They handle change better than most but need reassurance afterward.
- They alternate between energetic bursts and deep contemplation.

Balance: Engage their curiosity with enrichment like puzzle feeders, gentle challenges, and rotating toys, while protecting quiet spaces for reflection.

Wise One - Sensitive Soul (W/S): The Empathic Observer

Core Drive: To understand and harmonize.

These cats are the emotional anchors of the household. They sense moods, read the room, and often comfort both humans and other animals without being asked.

You'll see:

- They keep a calm distance but always remain nearby when someone's upset.
- Their gaze feels knowing; they seem to "read" emotion rather than behavior.
- They retreat if energy rises too high, only to return when calm is restored.

Balance: Keep their environment steady and emotionally predictable. When overwhelmed, they need stillness, not stimulation.

Sensitive Soul - Protector (S/P): The Gentle Guardian

Core Drive: To create emotional and physical safety for those they love.

This blend combines the empathy of the Sensitive Soul with the loyalty of the Protector. They are nurturing, protective, and quietly courageous.

You'll see:

- They comfort other pets or children in distress.
- They follow you closely when your energy shifts, showing a mix of worry and care.
- They may hide their own stress to stay "strong" for the family.

Balance: Let them know they don't have to manage the world. Gentle reassurance and steady affection remind them that you are their protector, too.

Adventurer - Sensitive Soul (A/S): The Passionate Companion

Core Drive: To connect through experience.

They're playful and social, but their heart leads as much as their curiosity. They might leap into your lap mid-game or press their face into your hand after exploring a new space, combining exuberance with tenderness.

You'll see:

- They recover quickly from stress when near their person.
- They form strong attachments and want to "share" experiences.
- They alternate between independent play and affectionate bursts.

Balance: Engage their energy with shared adventures like supervised outdoor walks, gentle training, or interactive play that satisfies both their heart and spirit.

How to Identify a Blend

If you're unsure whether your cat is a blend, ask yourself:

1. *Which type describes their motivation?*
   - What drives their actions: safety, curiosity, understanding, or connection?
2. *Which type describes their expression?*
   - How do they show that drive: boldly, thoughtfully, gently, or protectively?

A Protector-Adventurer, for example, is driven by safety (P) but expresses it through exploration (A). A Wise-Sensitive cat seeks understanding (W) but expresses it through empathy (S).

The first letter is your cat's core type, the "why." The second letter is their outward style, the "how."

The Emotional Advantage of Blended Cats

Blended-type cats are often the most emotionally balanced companions. They can adapt to changing dynamics, comfort others, and maintain harmony across personality differences. They act as emotional translators, which is the bridge between bolder and softer types.

In multi-cat homes, blended cats are often the social glue, patient with the shy, tolerant with the bold, and grounding for the anxious. Their emotional flexibility makes them invaluable teachers in compassion and coexistence.

Embracing the Spectrum

The beauty of the **P.A.W.S. Framework** isn't in classification but in compassion. Once you recognize that your cat's complexity mirrors your own, something profound happens: your relationship becomes a dialogue of respect, not expectation.

Your cat is not inconsistent for changing moods, but is communicating in the only way they know how. Every blend tells a story of growth, resilience, and trust: the Protector who learned to love, the Sensitive Soul who found courage, the Adventurer who discovered wisdom.

In their evolving personalities, we see our own capacity to adapt, heal, and become whole.

CHAPTER 8

LESSONS FROM THE LITTER BOX

WHAT CATS TEACH US ABOUT OURSELVES

No book about cats would be complete without a discussion of the litter box! If you live with a cat long enough, you will realize that the lessons they offer go far beyond purrs and play. They teach us patience, boundaries, and emotional truth. They reveal that comfort and cleanliness are about peace. And sometimes, their simplest actions, like stepping into the litter box, tell us more about emotional health than words ever could.

The litter box, often overlooked as mundane, is one of the most honest windows into a cat's emotional ecosystem. How your cat uses it, avoids it, or reacts around it speaks volumes about trust, control, safety, and balance, the same elements that shape our own relationships and self-care.

The Litter Box as a Mirror of Emotion

For a cat, the litter box is far more than a bathroom. It is a mirror of emotional truth. It's a space where instinct meets vulnerability, where boundaries are tested, and where comfort is quietly negotiated.

Cats use their litter box when they feel safe, unseen, and in control. That tiny corner of the home becomes a sacred zone, a place of release, privacy, and trust. In feline psychology, these moments are rituals of regulation: opportunities to express calm, reclaim territory, and reset balance.

But when safety wavers, energy in a home changes, schedules shift, another pet intrudes, or when the emotional climate turns tense, the litter box is often the first place to show the disturbance.

Behavior that humans dismiss as "acting out" is, in reality, a form of emotional communication. Cats don't protest; they manifest. Their behavior in the box tells us exactly how safe or unseen they feel.

Emotional Honesty in Four Forms

Through the **P.A.W.S. Framework**, we see that each personality type reveals its emotional truth in a distinct way:

- *The Protector:*
  - For the Protector, the litter box is sacred territory, a place that must remain predictable and private. They guard it instinctively, resisting sharing or any disruption to their pattern. Their behavior says, "If I control my space, I control my peace." When they begin to mark elsewhere or grow defensive, it's a plea for stability.
- *The Adventurer:*
  - For the Adventurer, curiosity and confidence shape everything. They may test new spots, try different substrates, or "go rogue" when something in the environment piques interest. Their actions say, "I wonder what happens if I try this instead." They remind

us that not all change is rebellion; sometimes it's exploration in disguise.

- *The Wise One:*
  - The Wise One approaches with calm calculation. They pause, observe, and wait for the world to feel safe. Their litter box ritual is measured, precise, deliberate, and full of awareness. If something feels "off," they hesitate rather than misbehave, and their silence teaches mindfulness: to pause, perceive, and proceed with intention.
- *The Sensitive Soul:*
  - For the Sensitive Soul, the litter box is an emotional sanctuary. Any tension, like raised voices, loud noises, or unfamiliar energy, can make that sanctuary feel unsafe. They may avoid it, hide, or choose another space entirely. Their message isn't disobedience; it's distress. They are saying, "The energy here feels heavy; I need gentleness before I can return."

What These Patterns Reveal

Each cat's behavior, though subtle, is deeply sincere, and every shift has meaning. Their patterns reflect not rebellion, but relationship. When we learn to read those small signs like an extra pause, a missed step, a new spot, we begin to understand their emotional map.

And what's most profound is this: the same principle applies to us.

Our own emotional well-being reveals itself through routine:

- When we feel safe, our days flow easily.
- When something inside us is unsettled, our habits, like sleep, diet, and focus, begin to show it first.

Just as a cat's litter box routine reflects their trust in the world, our daily rituals reflect our trust in ourselves.

Every clean scoop, every careful bury, every quiet pause is their way of restoring order within, an instinct we, too, can reclaim. If we tend our emotional litter box, the space where we release, reset, and renew, with the same care and neutrality that cats do, we become lighter, freer, and more in tune with the quiet rhythm of emotional health.

The P.A.W.S. Framework in the Litter Box

Let's look through the **P.A.W.S. lens** at how each personality type approaches this most personal behavior and what that reveals about both feline and human emotion.

The Protector: Boundaries as Safety

Primary Drive: To create order and control in their space.

Protectors treat the litter box as territory. They want predictability - the same box, in the same place, with the same substrate. A disruption, such as a new litter, a new location, or another cat intruding, can feel like an emotional invasion.

Their message: "I need structure to feel safe."

Human Reflection: Protectors remind us that setting boundaries has less to do with rigidity and more to do with emotional hygiene. Just as a cat won't share a litter box when they feel threatened, we too must protect our emotional spaces from chaos, clutter, and disrespect. Order is about peace of mind.

The Adventurer: Change as Curiosity

Primary Drive: To explore and experience new things.

Adventurers may test the limits, occasionally missing the box, digging with zeal, or trying out fresh locations. These actions are not an indication of misbehavior but a desire to experiment. They're asking, "What happens if I try it this way?"

Human Reflection: Adventurers remind us to stay curious even about our routines. Growth often requires messiness, the willingness to explore without shame. Their boldness in play and exploration teaches us that mistakes are not failures but data. Sometimes, you have to kick a little litter around to discover what feels right.

The Wise One: Observation Before Action

Primary Drive: To understand and make thoughtful choices.

Wise Ones are methodical. They approach the box calmly, ensuring safety and privacy before using it. They are precise, deliberate in covering, and tidy in rhythm. When that rhythm changes, it's always meaningful.

Human Reflection: Wise Ones remind us that observation is wisdom. In our lives, reflection often precedes right action. Like them, we thrive when we pause to assess before reacting. A clean space, physical or emotional, reflects clarity of mind.

The Sensitive Soul: Emotion as Environment

Primary Drive: To connect and harmonize.

Sensitive Souls are the emotional barometers of the home. A raised voice, a tense argument, or a change in energy can make them withdraw, sometimes avoiding the box entirely when overwhelmed. It's never spite; it's sensitivity.

Human Reflection: These cats teach us that emotional safety is as vital as physical safety. When our environment feels tense, our own "routines" like sleep, focus, and creativity often falter too.

When the Box Becomes a Barometer

In every home, the litter box tells the truth before anything else does. A Protector's guarding, an Adventurer's experimentation, a Wise One's precision, or a Sensitive Soul's withdrawal, these are emotional indicators.

The **P.A.W.S. Framework** helps decode them. A sudden change in litter behavior signals both physical discomfort and emotional imbalance. It reminds us to ask: What's shifted in their world or mine?

Lessons for the Human Heart

Before diving deeper, it helps to see the big picture. Just as cats instinctively teach us through their behavior, each P.A.W.S. type carries a quiet lesson for the human heart. The chart below translates these feline truths into human insights, illustrating how boundaries, curiosity, stillness, and emotional safety build healthier relationships, deeper self-awareness, and more intentional living. Each type teaches us a universal truth:

Type	Feline lesson:	Human reflection:
Protector (P)	Boundaries create peace.	Structure and consistency protect emotional stability.
Adventurer (A)	Exploration deepens understanding.	Curiosity expands comfort zones; mistakes are growth.
Wise One (W)	Stillness precedes clarity.	Mindfulness before reaction keeps relationships healthy.
Sensitive Soul (S)	Safety nurtures authenticity.	Emotional awareness is the foundation of empathy.

These aren't just traits; they're philosophies.

Cats live them instinctively, and we must learn them deliberately.

The Spiritual Lesson of the Litter Box

The litter box, in all its ordinary practicality, is really a temple of honesty. It's where cats release, reset, and reclaim balance, something we, too, are called to do in our emotional lives.

When a cat steps into their box, they do so without shame. They don't judge their needs, hide their natural rhythms, or apologize for existing. They do what must be done, then move on, clean, light, and free.

That's the quiet wisdom they offer us: to tend our inner world with the same neutrality - to cleanse, to forgive, to let go of what no longer serves, and to emerge ready for life again.

The **P.A.W.S. Framework** helps us interpret feline personality, but it also invites us to explore our own.

Are we Protectors, building a structure to feel safe?

Adventurers, learning by daring?

Wise Ones, pausing before we act?

Or Sensitive Souls, feeling the world too deeply?

Maybe, like our cats, we are blends, learning to balance order and curiosity, courage and calm, or empathy and discernment.

The litter box is a metaphor for what's unspoken. It is a place where comfort, control, and emotion quietly meet. When we honor our cat's rhythms there, we honor the truth that emotional balance begins in the spaces we tend to every day.

 CHAPTER 9

CREATING A HOME FOR EVERY TYPE

Every cat speaks through their surroundings. The way they walk into a room, claim a perch, hide beneath a blanket, or watch from a window. It's all part of their emotional conversation with the world. A cat's home is more than walls and furniture. It's an ecosystem of trust, rhythm, and energy. And just like people, cats thrive when their world reflects who they are inside.

Using the **P.A.W.S. Framework**, we can design spaces that align with each personality's emotional drive, whether that's Protection, Adventure, Wisdom, or Sensitivity.

When a home honors your cat's inner type, behavior improves naturally, anxiety eases, confidence grows, and connection deepens.

The Philosophy of an Emotionally Aligned Home

Every cat needs the same basic elements: safety, stimulation, rest, and routine, but each type experiences those elements differently.

- **Protectors** seek order and structure.
- **Adventurers** crave novelty and movement.
- **Wise Ones** value observation and quiet mastery.
- **Sensitive Souls** need calm and emotional resonance.

When these needs go unmet, behavioral challenges like scratching, avoidance, aggression, and withdrawal arise. But when their inner world is supported by their outer one, harmony returns.

Creating a home for every type begins with one simple question: "What does emotional safety mean for this cat?"

The Protector: Safe, Structured, Sovereign

Protectors thrive in spaces that feel predictable and organized. They are territorial, confident, and loyal, which makes them natural home guardians who feel responsible for stability.

Designing for the Protector:

- *Define Territory:* Give them vantage points where they can see but not be seen. These may be high perches, cat trees, or window shelves with a full view of their "kingdom."
- *Consistent Layout*: Avoid frequent rearranging of furniture or moving litter boxes and feeding stations. Change equals threat.
- *Controlled Access:* Provide quiet escape spaces (like a hooded bed or covered crate) where they can retreat and regulate stimulation.
- *Structured Play:* Play at predictable times each day; routine builds confidence.

Tone of the Home: Calm, orderly, and stable, i.e., a space where they can exhale without surprise.

Human Lesson: Protectors teach us that boundaries bring peace. Consistency is not confinement but kindness.

The Adventurer: Dynamic, Playful, Engaged

Adventurers are the bold spirits. These are the cats who leap before they look, chase before they calculate, and turn every corner into discovery. They thrive on variety and stimulation, but need grounding to balance their energy.

Designing for the Adventurer:

- *Vertical Freedom:* Cat trees, climbing shelves, and safe ledges give them elevation and excitement.
- *Rotating Toys:* Introduce new textures, scents, and puzzles every few days to satisfy curiosity.
- *Safe Outdoor Options:* Harness training, catios, or window perches satisfy their explorer instincts safely.
- *Interactive Playtime:* Laser toys, feather wands, and tunnels create shared adventure, which is their love language.
- *"Yes Zones":* Designate play areas where exploration is encouraged, so boundaries don't feel restrictive.

Tone of the Home: Stimulating but secure, which is alive with movement but rooted in safety.

Human Lesson: Adventurers remind us that joy comes from curiosity. Growth requires space to play, even for grown-ups.

The Wise One: Still, Observant, Discerning

Wise Ones are the philosophers of the feline world. They observe first, act later, and bring balance wherever they reside. They prefer calm over chaos, contemplation over commotion.

Designing for the Wise One:

- *Quiet Sanctuaries:* Provide cozy nooks away from traffic, like behind couches, under beds, or near warm lamps.
- *Observation Points*: Window perches where they can watch birds or the household rhythm from a distance.
- *Gentle Lighting*: Soft, warm tones reduce stress and mirror their peaceful nature.
- *Pacing & Routine*: Maintain a slow, predictable rhythm; abrupt noise or change feels jarring.
- *Enrichment through Subtlety*: Puzzle feeders or scent-based toys let them engage their intellect quietly.

Tone of the Home: Peaceful, contemplative, and predictable, a library of calm in a noisy world.

Human Lesson: Wise Ones teach us to create spaces that support reflection. Stillness isn't emptiness, but emotional clarity.

The Sensitive Soul: Gentle, Emotional, Harmonious

Sensitive Souls feel everything from the tone of your voice, the mood of a room, and even the energy between other pets. They need homes that whisper calmness and consistency.

Designing for the Sensitive Soul:

- *Soft Spaces:* Use plush textures, blankets, and low lighting to soften sensory input.
- *Predictable Energy*: Keep routines gentle and voices low; they read emotional tone as safety.

- *Private Refuge:* Create a "peace corner", a spot they can retreat to when the world feels too loud.
- *Music & Scent Therapy:* Soft classical music, diffused cat-safe lavender, or heartbeat pillows can soothe their nervous systems.
- *Gentle Interaction*: Let them approach you. Offer calm presence, not pursuit.

Tone of the Home: Warm, quiet, and emotionally transparent, a sanctuary for sensitivity.

Human Lesson: Sensitive Souls remind us that tenderness is strength. The more safety we create, the more love returns.

Blended Homes for Blended Cats

Most cats express a blend of types, and so should their environments.

- A Protector/Adventurer (P/A) needs structured safety and dynamic play. Give them predictable playtimes and a secure "command center" perch.
- A Wise/Sensitive (W/S) cat thrives in peaceful spaces filled with emotional consistency. Keep routines gentle, and ensure they have calm, private retreats.
- A Sensitive/Protector (S/P) benefits from warmth and reassurance, plus a clear household structure.
- An Adventurer/Wise One (A/W) enjoys interactive play balanced with quiet observation spaces.

When designing for blended cats, always prioritize their primary drive: the "why" behind their behavior, and then layer in the secondary type's expression style.

Example: If your cat is a Sensitive (primary) who expresses as a Protector, focus on emotional calm first, structure second.

The Energy of the Home

Cats don't separate emotional energy from physical space. For them, they're the same thing.

A cluttered, chaotic home breeds overstimulation; a lifeless home dulls curiosity. The goal isn't silence or order but balance.

To create harmony for any type:

- Keep daily rhythms predictable.
- Manage your own tone and movements.
- Respect their need for privacy and choice.
- Use your voice and presence as emotional architecture: calm, gentle, and attuned.

Your energy is the blueprint for your cat's environment.

 # CHAPTER 10

CLOSING REFLECTIONS

HOW OUR CATS SHAPE OUR HUMANITY

At the start of this journey, we wanted to learn our cats' language, that is, to read their signals, understand their moods, and bring more peace into our homes. But somewhere along the way, something remarkable happened: we realized they've been teaching us how to live, love, and lead with more grace.

Cats shape us, quietly, consistently, and profoundly. They slow our pace, sharpen our awareness, and remind us that emotional honesty doesn't need words.

Through the **P.A.W.S. Framework**, we learned to categorize feline behavior and witnessed emotional intelligence in its purest form. Each type, the Protector, Adventurer, Wise One, and Sensitive Soul, holds a mirror to a part of the human heart, revealing the ways we protect, explore, reflect, and feel.

The P.A.W.S. Mirror: What Cats Reflect Back to Us

Our cats are more than companions. They are living metaphors of human truth.

Every flick of a tail, every pause before a leap, every moment of retreat or affection carries a reflection of something ancient and familiar: *ourselves.*

We like to think we're the observers, studying our cats. But those who live closely with them know the quiet truth: they're observing us, too. And through their presence, they reflect back the emotional language we've forgotten how to speak: patience, boundaries, curiosity, trust, and the art of simply being.

The **P.A.W.S. Framework** isn't just a way to understand cats.

It's a mirror. One that reveals how our own inner world interacts with theirs.

Each type embodies a core emotional truth that calls something forward in us, something we need to remember, practice, or heal.

When we look deeply at our cats, we don't just learn who they are. We learn who we are becoming.

The Protector: The Mirror of Boundaries and Trust

Protectors are the keepers of order, guardians of peace, stewards of structure. In their quiet vigilance, they hold a mirror to our human relationship with control, safety, and responsibility.

Protector cats walk their territory with intention. They memorize every sound, every scent, every rhythm of the home. Their confidence comes not from dominance, but from knowing the rules of their world. They feel safest when life follows a pattern they can trust.

When they guard a doorway, patrol their favorite perch, or bristle at an unexpected visitor, they aren't being possessive; instead, they are defending the stability that helps them feel secure. And in doing so, they invite us to look at how we, too, protect our inner worlds.

We all have a Protector within us, which is the part that builds boundaries, maintains order, and resists change when life feels uncertain. Some call it control. But in truth, it's care. It's the instinct to keep chaos out and calm in.

Through the **P.A.W.S. lens**, the Protector's drive for safety reflects one of the deepest emotional truths in both species: that peace isn't the absence of boundaries but the presence of reliable structure.

Their routines remind us that predictability is not dull; it's healing.

That discipline can be an act of love.

And that protecting something, whether a home, a heart, or a habit, is not about power, but about peace.

What They Mirror in Us:

- The human need for stability and routine.
- The importance of saying no without guilt.
- The wisdom of safeguarding what gives us peace.

Human Reflection:

Protectors remind us that boundaries are not walls but bridges, structures that allow us to meet safely in the middle. They teach us that protecting our energy, time, and emotional well-being is not selfishness; it's stewardship.

When we, like them, learn to stand calmly in our space and hold what matters with care, we stop confusing control with love and begin to see both as partners in harmony.

The Adventurer: The Mirror of Courage and Curiosity

If the Protector represents the home's heart, the Adventurer is its wings.

The Adventurer cat is the fearless explorer, the joyful risk-taker, the student of the unknown.

They are the embodiment of curiosity unclouded by fear, an energy that expands the world rather than resists it.

They leap before hesitation wins. They investigate every new sound, new scent, new opportunity. For them, life is not a territory to control, but a mystery to engage.

When an Adventurer scales the bookshelf or slips through a half-open door, it isn't defiance, but the feline expression of wonder. They teach us that curiosity is the root of confidence, and that safety, paradoxically, grows when we trust ourselves enough to take a leap.

Through the **P.A.W.S. Framework**, the Adventurer represents the drive to experience and expand, which is the same drive that fuels human growth. They remind us that the edges of comfort are not walls but gateways, and that joy is found not in knowing, but in discovering.

In their boldness, we see our own dormant courage: the version of ourselves that once reached without fear, that played without purpose, that believed the world was good and worth exploring.

Their playful daring asks us:

"When was the last time you tried something new, not to succeed, but to feel alive?"

Because every leap, every sniff of new air, every chase of a shadow carries the same message:

That motion heals stagnation, and that the world expands as we do.

"The Adventurer shows us that joy is not found in certainty, but discovered in motion."

What They Mirror in Us:

- The human need for discovery and challenge.
- The courage to risk without fearing failure.
- The reminder that life's vitality lies beyond repetition.

Human Reflection:

The Adventurer teaches us that curiosity is not chaos; it's trust in self.

We grow most when we dare, play, and explore without demanding an outcome.

They reveal that courage is not the absence of fear, but the willingness to meet it with wonder.

When we live like Adventurers, we don't abandon safety; we expand it.

We build confidence not from control, but from movement.

The Wise One: The Mirror of Stillness and Discernment

The Wise One is the quiet center of the feline world, the philosopher in fur, the monk in the sunlight, the observer who knows when to move and when to wait. Through them, we glimpse our own capacity for patience, discernment, and mindfulness.

A Wise One doesn't rush to act. They study the moment with eyes half-closed, tail wrapped neatly around still paws, as though the world is revealing itself one breath at a time. Their calm is not passivity, but it is mastery. They show us that awareness itself is a form of strength.

When the room grows loud, the Wise One withdraws, not out of fear, but to preserve inner equilibrium, and when life becomes chaotic, they choose stillness, not to escape, but for clarity.

Their rhythm mirrors what humans often forget in the rush of modern life: that wisdom is not about knowing everything, but about not needing to. Their restraint teaches emotional discipline, and their silence teaches presence. Through their eyes, we rediscover the lost art of observation.

What They Mirror in Us:

- The power of observation before action.
- The value of solitude in emotional restoration.
- The beauty of understanding without control.

Human Reflection:

Wise Ones remind us that clarity doesn't arrive through reaction, but through reflection. They mirror the parts of us that crave balance in a world that glorifies busyness and show that peace isn't found by avoiding the world, but by standing calmly inside it.

When we live in their rhythm, we learn to listen before speaking, to pause before choosing, to act from awareness rather than impulse. In their silence, we find wisdom; in their gaze, perspective.

The Sensitive Soul: The Mirror of Empathy and Emotional Truth

The Sensitive Soul is the heart of the **P.A.W.S. Framework** - the empath, the healer, the soft vibration that attunes to everything unspoken. They are living barometers of energy. The shift of a tone, a sigh, a silence. They feel it all.

For them, emotion is environment. When peace reigns, they blossom; when tension lingers, they withdraw. Their tenderness is not weakness; it is language. It is their way of saying, "I feel with you."

They remind us of the profound truth that sensitivity is not fragility, but the soul's radar.

Through their reactions, we see the invisible architecture of our own emotional landscapes.

When a Sensitive Soul hides during conflict or presses their forehead against your hand after a long day, they're teaching empathy in its truest form: empathy as presence, not performance.

They mirror the quiet part of us that feels deeply but rarely speaks it aloud.

The Sensitive Soul teaches that gentleness is a form of strength, and that love, to be real, must feel safe.

What They Mirror in Us:

- The courage to feel without apology.
- The need to create calm before connection.
- The reminder that emotional safety is sacred.

Human Reflection:

The Sensitive Soul teaches us to stop seeing empathy as a burden and start seeing it as a superpower. They reveal that awareness of emotion, ours or others', is not an inconvenience but intelligence in its most intuitive form.

The Circle of Trust

Every relationship with a cat begins as a slow, graceful circle: a dance of approach and retreat, curiosity and caution. It starts with two living beings learning to breathe in unison.

At first, that circle may feel fragile.

You offer care: food, warmth, a soft voice.

They offer watchfulness: studying your tone, your movement, your energy. Each moment of calm, each blink of safety, draws the circle closer.

Trust, in the feline world, is not taken; it's earned in whispers. It's built in the pauses, not the performances; in silence, not insistence.

Over time, that circle stops being about ownership and becomes companionship. You don't possess your cat; you participate in their peace. You learn that love, for them, is not a display of affection, but an atmosphere. They live in your energy, not your words.

Through that silent exchange, they begin to mirror you.

Your calm becomes their calm.
Your tension becomes their distance.
Your consistency becomes their confidence.

They feel your moods, your silence, your presence, and respond to who you are, not what you do. They don't love you because you feed them or entertain them; they love you because you create safety. You speak the Language of P.A.W.S. not with words, but with the constancy of being.

The P.A.W.S. Framework and the Circle of Trust

Each **P.A.W.S.** type enters and maintains the circle of trust differently, teaching us that relationships are never one-size-fits-all.

- **Protector (P)** - Trust through structure.
  - They need routine, predictability, and respect for boundaries. Every consistent moment says, "You are safe with me." They teach that reliability is love in action.
- **Adventurer (A)** - Trust through shared experience.
  - They bond through interaction and play, learning who you are by exploring with you. They show that trust grows not from control, but from curiosity.

- **Wise One (W)** - Trust through observation.
  - They watch quietly before engaging, testing your patience and presence. They teach that understanding must precede closeness and that space is not rejection, but respect.
- **Sensitive Soul (S)** - Trust through energy.
  - They attune to your emotional state before your physical touch. They need calm, consistency, and gentleness. They teach that emotional safety is the deepest form of love.

When we meet a cat where they are, whether in their natural rhythm or at their emotional temperature, we close the circle. And when that happens, something ancient and sacred stirs: two species moving in harmony, united by a shared emotional language older than words.

Living Within the Circle of Trust

To live inside the circle of trust with a cat is to experience a relationship stripped to its essence: no pretense, no performance, no condition.

It's the kind of connection humans often crave but rarely achieve: simple, mutual, and profoundly honest.

Your cat doesn't ask you to be cheerful, productive, or perfect.

They ask you to be consistent. To show up in your true energy, to mean what you do, and to do it with gentleness.

They don't want your constant attention; they want your calm attention.

They don't need endless affection; they need emotional alignment.

When you live this way, you begin to see how the same circle exists in every human relationship too: with partners, children, friends, colleagues.

Trust begins not with doing more, but with being steady.

Safety, once created, becomes the soil where connection grows.

Reflection: The Human Lesson

The Circle of Trust is the emotional legacy of the **P.A.W.S. Framework**, the living result of empathy in practice. It's the proof that connection doesn't come from understanding behavior alone, but from understanding the emotion beneath it.

Your cat doesn't need perfection.
They need predictability.
They need presence.
They need peace.

And perhaps so do you.

When you learn to create safety for your cat, you're also learning to create safety within yourself: to listen instead of rush, to protect without control, to love without demand.

In doing so, you become a gentler version of yourself, and that, in the end, is their greatest gift.

ONE FINAL REQUEST

You've reached the end of this journey, through P.A.W.S and personalities, instincts and insight, lessons from the litter box, and the quiet ways our cats shape who we become.

By now, you've seen that this book isn't really just about cats. It's about understanding behavior with compassion, honoring differences, and creating spaces at home and within ourselves, where every personality can feel safe, respected, and seen.

If The Secret Language of P.A.W.S has helped you deepen your bond with your cat, shift how you interpret behavior, or reflect on your own emotional patterns, I would be sincerely grateful if you'd take a moment to leave a review.

Your words, whether a few sentences or a short paragraph, help other readers find this book and decide if it's right for them. Sharing what resonated, which chapter stayed with you, or how your perspective changed can make a meaningful difference.

Thank you for reading, for reflecting, and for listening so closely to the quiet language our cats have been speaking all along.

With appreciation,

- J.W. Kincaid

Scan QR code below to download Appendices. The Payhip website collects email addresses for the BenG. Publishing email list. You can opt out at any time.

FURTHER READING

The Cat Purrsonality Test: What Our Feline Friends Are Really Thinking / Alison Davies, 2021. Summary: fun way to demystify your pet's mysterious mind by answering 81 multiple choice questions.

Is Your Cat a Psychopath?: A Personality Quiz Book to Find Out If Your Cat Is Pussolini or Mother Purresa / Steven Wildish, 2023. Summary: A humorous personality quiz book to determine if your cat is secretly plotting world domination or spreading peace, complete with 16 profiles and tips for cat-human harmony.

The *cat behavior* answer book : understanding how *cats* think, why they do what they do, and how to strengthen our relationships with them / Arden Moore, 2022. Summary: Moore answers the many questions cat owners have, from the practical aspects of training, feeding, and caring to the puzzling aspects of behavior and communication.

Cat Astrology: Decode your pet's personality with the power of the zodiac / Stella Andromeda, 2021. *Summary*: A guide to understanding your cat's personality through zodiac signs, offering insights into pet-owner compatibility and astrological traits of different feline sun signs.

Just for Fun

Cats and Kittens Coloring [series] / Ben G. Publishing, 2025. *Summary*: festive coloring books for cat lovers featuring simple illustrations of kittens in fun and relaxing scenes for a variety of holidays. Suitable for all ages.

REFERENCES

Amat, M., Camps, T., & Manteca, X. (2016). Behavior problems in cats: Evaluation and management. *Journal of Veterinary Behavior, 15*, 1–7.

Arahori, M., Kuroshima, H., Hori, Y., & Fujita, K. (2016). Owners' view of their pets' emotions, cognition, and behavior: A comparison between dogs and cats. *Animal Cognition, 20*, 1–16.

Arahori, M., Kuroshima, H., Hori, Y., Takagi, S., & Fujita, K. (2017). Owners' view of their cats' emotions, behavior, and cognitive abilities: A cross-cultural study between Japan and the United States. *Anthrozoös, 30*(3), 361–375.

Bradshaw, J. W. S. (2013). *Cat sense: How the new feline science can make you a better friend to your pet*. Basic Books.

Bradshaw, J. W. S., Casey, R. A., & Brown, S. L. (2012). *The behavior of the domestic cat* (2nd ed.). CABI.

Curtis, T. M., Knowles, R. J., Crowell-Davis, S. L., & McCobb, E. (2003). Influence of familiarity and relatedness on proximity and allogrooming in domestic cats (*Felis catus*). *American Journal of Veterinary Research, 64*(9), 1151–1154.

Edwards, C., Heiblum, M., Tejeda, A., & Galindo, F. (2007). Experimental evaluation of attachment behaviors in owned cats. *Journal of Veterinary Behavior, 2*(3), 119–125.

Edwards, C., & Cameron-Beattie, M. (2017). Understanding subtle feline social cues. *Applied Animal Behaviour Science, 194*, 86–93.

Ellis, S. L. H. (2009). Enrichment and play needs of indoor cats. *Veterinary Clinics of North America: Small Animal Practice, 39*(2), 359–369.

Ellis, S. L., & Wells, D. L. (2010). The influence of housing conditions on the behavior and welfare of domestic cats. *Animal Welfare, 19*, 303–312.

Feldman, H. N. (1994). Domestic cat home ranges and social organization. *Anthrozoös, 7*(3), 171–186.

Feuerstein, N., & Terkel, J. (2008). Interrelationships of dogs (*Canis familiaris*) and cats (*Felis catus*) living under the same roof. *Applied Animal Behaviour Science, 113*(1–3), 150–165.

Galvan, M., & Vonk, J. (2016). Man's other best friend: Domestic cats (*Felis catus*) and their discrimination of human emotion cues. *Animal Cognition, 19*(1), 193–205.

Gosling, S. D. (2001). From mice to men: What can we learn about personality from animal research? *Psychological Bulletin, 127*(1), 45–86.

Gosling, S. D., Kwan, V. S. Y., & John, O. P. (2003). A dog's got personality: A cross-species comparative approach to personality judgments in dogs and cats. *Journal of Personality and Social Psychology, 85*(6), 1161–1169.

Jones, A. C., & Gosling, S. D. (2005). Temperament and personality in dogs and cats. In J. Serpell (Ed.), *The domestic dog: Its evolution, behavior and interactions with people* (pp. 110–130). Cambridge University Press.

Leech, L. E., Hampson, S., & McGreevy, P. (2022). The effects of owner and domestic cat (*Felis catus*) demographics on personality traits. *Applied Animal Behaviour Science.*

Litchfield, C. A., Quinton, G., Tindle, H., Chiera, B., Kikillus, K. H., & Roetman, P. (2017). The "Feline Five": An exploration of personality in pet cats (*Felis catus*). *PLOS ONE, 12*(8), e0183455.

Mikkola, S., Salonen, M., Hakanen, E., Sulkama, S., & Lohi, H. (2021). Reliability and validity of seven feline behaviour and personality traits. *Animals, 11*(7), 1991.

Quaranta, A., d'Ingeo, S., Amoruso, R., & Siniscalchi, M. (2020). Emotion recognition in cats. *Animal Cognition, 23*, 1131–1141.

Rochlitz, I. (2007). The impact of environment on feline territorial behavior. *Journal of Feline Medicine and Surgery, 9*(5), 402–413.

Sparkes, A. H. (2013). Feline sickness behavior: Subtle signs and monitoring. *Journal of Feline Medicine and Surgery, 15*(5), 389–403.

Stella, J., & Croney, C. (2016). Environmental stress in cats. *Journal of Feline Medicine and Surgery, 18*(10), 776–783.

Stella, J., Croney, C., & Buffington, T. (2014). Environmental factors that affect the behavior and welfare of domestic cats in the home. *Journal of Feline Medicine and Surgery, 16*(8), 693–702.

Takagi, S., Arahori, M., Chijiiwa, H., Saito, A., Kuroshima, H., Hori, Y., & Fujita, K. (2019). There's no ball without noise: Cats' prediction of object location from sounds. *Animal Cognition, 22*, 981–992.

Turner, D. C. (2017). A review of over three decades of research on cat–human and human–cat interactions and relationships. *Behavioural Processes, 141*, 297–304.

Turner, D. C., & Bateson, P. (Eds.). (2014). *The domestic cat: The biology of its behaviour* (3rd ed.). Cambridge University Press.

Vitale, K. R., Behnke, A. C., & Udell, M. A. R. (2019). Attachment bonds between domestic cats and humans. *Current Biology, 29*(18), R864–R865.

Vitale, K. R., & Udell, M. A. R. (2019). Adult domestic cats (*Felis catus*) show improved social learning in the presence of a bonded human partner. *Animal Cognition, 22*(3), 453–462.

FOLLOW BEN G. PUBLISHING ON SOCIAL MEDIA!

Website

Amazon

Facebook

Instagram

Tiktok